THE OWNER
of the TREASURE

The
OWNER
of the TREASURE

DOMINIK V. FREY

Library of Congress Control Number:		2016912499
ISBN:	Hardcover	978-1-5245-2948-2
	Softcover	978-1-5245-2947-5
	eBook	978-1-5245-2977-2

Print information available on the last page.

Rev. date: 07/28/2016

To order additional copies of this book, contact:
Xlibris
1-888-795-4274
www.Xlibris.com
Orders@Xlibris.com
742928

The first thing a person must do if he wants to discover and later recover buried treasure is to make a pact with El Compadre, the odd name given in this part of the world to the Prince of Darkness, the devil, the demon, Satan, Beelzebub, or Lucifer—owner, according to shamanic and witchcraft tradition, of all buried treasure.

CONTENTS

DOMINIK V. FREY

Born in Mexico City in 1961, electromechanical engineer.

Like any young man of the sixties, he has been an adventurer and free spirit, making excursions to remote locations all over Mexico, especially those connected to mountaineering, such as the Popocatépetl, volcano he has climbed on several occasions. But his greatest adventure was to venture into the world of magic and witchcraft (placed at the service of treasure seekers), where anything might happen, as the reader will discover in this book.

Nothing is more exciting for anyone than to discover the secrets of buried treasure, and this soon became apparent to the author as the extraordinary events that unfolded during excavations became commonplace. The magic of the sites where these incidents occurred only added to the mystery.

As he participated in all this, he discovered that he has a special inner gift that helped him close the gap between reality and imagination. Unsolved mysteries are solved, and treasures that would have remained buried forever, discovered. This story flows from beginning to the end and is compelling reading from page 1.

DEDICATION

I dedicate this work with all my heart and soul to the people who have supported me selflessly in the good times and bad. I am referring to the doctors, engineers, architects, ranchers, and housewives, who through their economic, moral, and unconditional support have made this experience possible. It needs to be pointed out that the total sum of financial assistance during the two years of searching amounted to $20,000. I extend my heartfelt thanks to the people who have made this work possible through their support.

This story will be of interest to people with an enterprising and adventurous spirit; for nothing is written elsewhere about rites, esoteric powers, supernatural happenings, incantations, excavations, caves, and so on because many people who have attempted to salvage a treasure have died and others who have managed to enter and leave caves have been left mentally scarred by the experience.

Nevertheless, my greatest allegiance, respect, and love are reserved for the infinite and sublime being of the universe that has spared my life so that this story can be told. It is necessary to stress the great importance that my companions had in the playing out of this adventure. We all suffered the same hardships, but they trusted in me and stayed by my side. The feeling of unity, affection, and true friendship that was forged between us allowed us to advance and finally discover one of the greatest secrets there is in the search for treasure. For many people, this theme is taboo, but I trust that this book will serve as a stimulus and guide for those capable of accepting challenges and who have the will to pursue their dreams.

PROLOGUE

The events detailed in this book are absolutely true, and within the pages of this book many of life's mysteries are unveiled.

I am convinced that the theme of this experience will awaken your interest. The book's content is very strong and has been written in a manner that should help you avoid the dangers that the search for occult treasure entails. I had always been a believer and was committed to the word of God until the day in which this journey, which lasted two years, began.

Throughout this book, things that are not scientifically provable will be discovered, such as esotericism and its great inherent power. Supernatural cases are presented at different stages of the trek, impressive and unforgettable adventures that left their mark on the lives of those involved. There were accidents that afflicted us from time to time, falls suffered when climbing mountains, the destruction of a van attacked by wild pigs, the risks faced in wild zones infested with pythons larger than anacondas by ocelots and other wild animals. Many long nights were characterized by the appearance of elves and giant bats, and by day and night, we were hunted by native communities that live near enchanted places. All those incidents contributed to serious economic costs and threatened to call the excursions off.

My personal life was greatly affected by this adventure, resulting in the end of my marriage. There were so many things that happened to us that the question must be asked as to why we didn't call everything off in the beginning. The answer to that question is simple in that our exploration, searching, and discovery went beyond the limits that most would be prepared to go. Legends and treasure-hunting myths are familiar to most people, whether they be in caves, under the earth, on islands, in rivers, in wells, or even in the walls of houses. But coming face-to-face with those things is something else. Let me relate how the terrible adventure began when I went to live in La Huasteca Potosina, in the province of Tamazunchale, which means place of toads, a city whose main commercial activity is centered on beef and cultivation of oranges and coffee. It was here that I opened my bodywork and spray-painting workshop, which is still operating today, and began to get to know the people of the city soon after my arrival.

One day a man came to my workshop and offered to sell me a metal detector. I'm sure that you've heard many stories about people giving everything up to go and search for buried treasure, and here in the city of Tamazunchale, many have become millionaires overnight after falling upon a cache of treasure by accident (call it good luck if you like). Jars full of gold have been found on people's properties or discovered stashed in adobe walls in the process of remodeling or demolishing buildings.

There are also many surprising stories that are told by the locals that perhaps will no doubt seem like fiction, but I can assure you that these stories are true, and I will retell some of them shortly, but first let me explain why the city has such unbounded wealth.

One needs to go back to the days of the Mexican Revolution, when rumor had it that many armed groups like the Zapatistas, Villistas, or Carrancistas came to the area. Out of fear of losing the wealth they had accumulated, many buried their valuables under the earth or in the walls of their houses or in caves or wells. After the money and jewels were buried, thick layers of stone were tossed on top. Even soldiers hid their treasure (perhaps robbed in the first place) in caves, and there are some caches that contain period weapons as well.

Before I begin to relate the incredible journey that my group completed, I will introduce you to the individuals who shared this odyssey with me.

Thirteen people covered half of the costs, four used clairvoyance along the way, and three accompanied me and dug at my side. The financial support came from Dr. Vicente E. Franc, renowned gynecologist; Dr. Rich Olguin, general practitioner of the region of Huasteca; two housewives, Carla Roque and Guadalupe, both doctors' wives; a rancher, Mr. Torres Perez, a wealthy and powerful man of the region who also participated in the adventure; another rancher, Don Roque, who supported us financially and materially; a businessman from Mexico City, Mr. Rolando Guzman; the chief executive of Frontera buses, Señor Jose; the architect Sergio Guerrero; and Dr. Cata, country doctor in the Huexco community.

You might ask why so many backed us without expecting to receive anything in return. The answer is that they have worked their way up from humble beginnings and are aware of the risks involved. Many treasure seekers have died, perhaps as a result of overly enjoying the wealth they have discovered. Only through support and teamwork could the prospects of success be increased.

The question is why do people who discover buried treasure die? Is it because of the gases that deeply buried metal can produce or some other unfathomable reason that claims their lives? To be able to find that answer, we went through two years of hardship, but I consider the effort worthwhile because our inner values were put to the test. We found a way to survive and to bond with our fellow adventurers.

But who were these people who accompanied me to the high mountains and to incredible caves that very few have seen and even fewer have managed to leave alive?

Let me present Ms. Edilia Hernandez, a twenty-seven-year-old sociologist, and Hidalgo Ariel, thirty-eight years old, who works in the field of human relations. They were with me the last eight months; but before them, there were two others: Ms. Guadalupe, already mentioned above, and young Jesus Hernandez, a twenty-right-year-old salesman. These four people, with mystical powers, will be referred to frequently in the pages of this book. It needs to be pointed out that I got to know all of them slowly, and one of them also helped me develop the power of clairvoyance.

Each one of the adventures will be mentioned, the moment they took place, and the effect that the power of each one produced. At the end of the book, I will reveal the secret of how that power is released and the reason for its use. I will also detail the secret of how to dig a treasure up.

All this is very personal. If one wants to participate in an adventure in the secret search for riches, it needs to be thought through in advance over and over. Is it a simple thing to unearth treasure? I can assure you that it isn't, which means that much thought is needed before committing yourself to take the final step because once started, avoiding the consequences is all but impossible.

At the end of these events, another person will be introduced, and it is through him that the final secret of success is found.

Let's start then with what happened, following a chronological order in which all these fantastic and incredible events took place.

1

Personal Discovery of an Abnormal Energy within Me

L
et's go back in time some twenty years to that moment when I visited San Luis Potosi for the first time. My wife, whom I met in Mexico City, was born in Tamazunchale, a town in this beautiful area; and it was thanks to her that I first set foot in the lands of Potosi. As I thought back to that time now, the impressions that that first experience awakened are still vivid in my mind.

The site that we arrived in was a small town called Tampacan, in Huasteca Potosina, and we stayed at the house of my wife's well-to-do uncle.

Huasteca Potosina landscape

After accommodating our things in the room, I went out for a walk around the town and soon discovered the great hospitality of the locals.

At dusk, the singing of dark-blue feathered birds called thrushes filled the air. Their song was so loud that sleep was impossible even though I felt extraordinarily calm and at peace with the world.

The cacophony returned at daybreak and made me feel as if we were in the center of a vast jungle. It was an unusual welcome to that mystical place, but as strange as it may sound, the song of the thrushes was assimilated into the depths of my being and eventually just became part of a typical day.

After living ten years there, I became somewhat of an expert on the region and made many friends with the humble and simple folk of the town and surrounding countryside. Everything, like the din of the birds, eventually became normal and predictable, save one thing: the high standard of living of just about everyone there.

This, of course, stirred my curiosity to ascertain what the source of such income could be.

My wife's family surprised me when they told me that the population's wealth had come from the discovery of buried treasure. Around that time, my wife's brother-in-law used to travel to San Luis Potosi; and when I relayed that message on to him, he urged me to invest in a device so we could go out and look for some treasure of our own. But I didn't pay him any attention; I was happy enough to listen to all the stories and had no desire to take it any further than that.

In the following five years, I heard one fascinating story after the next. Everyone talked openly about their odysseys and excavations. They were very detailed descriptions, which I took in as I limited myself to listening and respecting what I was told. The mention of the presence of the supernatural in all that, backed up by its verification, fascinated me.

I am a person who during one stage of my life belonged to a religion based on the highest biblical principles through which I gained an extensive knowledge of divine powers. I am also well informed about celestial powers that the myriad of demonic angels found on earth possess. Likewise, I know perfectly well that supernatural power that does not come from God is possessed by people who devote themselves to helping those with health or spiritual problems. Because of what I was told in the city and the way it was told to me, it was easy to see that many of the inhabitants were afraid. Nevertheless, I began to have my doubts that the events that had been described to me were, in fact, authentic.

In 1996, together with my family, we were in the process of making arrangements to settle in Tamazunchale. We were renting a house on the outskirts, ten minutes from the city, in a zone named Buenos Aires. I had barely lived a year in that place; but during that time, I organized two excursions into the beautiful surrounding landscape of Huasteca Potosina, in which all my friends from Mexico City participated.

Around the same time, I was invited to go on my first treasure hunt. Unfortunately, I didn't have time to take part because I was busy with my spiritual duties as well as a backlog of repair work to do. I had taken advantage of the space in the yard behind the house I was renting to do some repairs for friends and my wife's relatives, and it seemed that the word had gotten around that I did a good job. A few more months and maybe I would have the first signs of a viable business.

However, our stay there was interrupted by the insistence of my wife to return to Mexico City. There had been problems in the marriage before we'd come to Tamazunchale, and in a way, those problems had prompted our decision to move in the first place. Nothing was very clear at the time; but perhaps those problems, rather than being solved by living in a small town, had been exacerbated instead. I couldn't complain about returning because it was my wife's town and her family that was living close to us. She didn't want to stay, and I had no alternative other than accompanying her back to the metropolis of Mexico City.

I felt a mix of emotions the day that we left Tamazunchale. I was attracted to the town and the life there for a reason that I couldn't understand very well at the time; there was something mystical that fascinated me about being there, and the possibility of building my own business added to that feeling of adventure. But I could see well enough that the marriage was heading nowhere good at the same time. Perhaps a second time around in Mexico City would be better.

When I'd arrived in the country, I also had some work selling products for an agricultural company; and when we returned to the city, a well-paid job for the same company came up in the United States. It was a chance to save money, and I talked it over with my wife and decided it would be a good idea to give it a try for a while.

But in the end, instead of living there a year alone, I finished up staying five years, returning to Mexico during the vacations. The money I sent home helped put the marriage on a better financial footing, and when I finally came back, we had put enough money together to think about buying our own house in Tamazunchale. Five years was a long time to live like that, and any bad memories that we'd had about living together before were more or less forgotten. I returned to Mexico in 2000 with the plan of moving definitively to Tamazunchale.

I bought a house and property in the same zone that I had previously lived in, thirty meters above the level of the road. To solve the problem of entering the property, I decided to contract machinery to clear the property; and every morning as I went about doing that, I would see a cowboy pass by, driving his cattle toward their pastures.

I started building a metal structure that was to serve as an office, but unfortunately, it only lasted two weeks before it was blown down by a fierce north wind.

The workshop before rebuilding.

Later, I reinforced the whole structure with mortar although my original idea was to build a water deposit because the area had no drinking water. My business was going well, and I had a lot of customers because of the high-quality service I offered. As well, the people who worked with me were very honest and were keen to learn more about the restoration of cars.

From my workshop, a small very old house could be seen, which, for some unknown reason, attracted my attention. After some time there, some of my customers began asking me if I wasn't afraid of working late into the night in such an isolated place. One day, one of them mentioned that the sound of a mystery rider on horseback could be heard around midnight in this part of the region. This rider had apparently galloped past startled people out walking at night.

On another occasion, someone else asked me if I took my tools home with me at night because I was afraid of them being stolen. I told him I'd never done that because I was on the property most of the time and would sense it if someone wanted to rob me.

My answer surprised the man who had asked the question. I wondered if he thought I was psychic or something like that. There was no doubt that he believed in the supernatural.

Some days later, another customer visited me to tell me he was sorry because he had tried to take my tools back to his house to do a repair. According to what he told me, on getting out of his car and setting foot on my property, all the loose pieces (chests, caskets, and other heavy iron objects) that were scattered around the workshop started lifting off the ground and fell heavily one after the other. Terrified, he charged back out of the workshop as fast as he could, only to find his own car badly damaged by a fallen rock. Days later, he developed a serious stomach complaint.

Because of the terrifying experience, he went to a local healer who told him that my workshop was located in an area protected by a spirit or energy and that I, in fact, was under the same protection. The healer, however, couldn't see that on the night of the incident that this protection was in place. As a result, word got around about what had happened, and I was treated with the utmost caution and respect from then on.

One day, while I was working, the cowhand Honorio Villegas stopped by to pay his respects. He wanted to know if what he'd heard was true. I told him that it was; and then he wanted to know if, given the circumstances, I wasn't afraid of working alone. He seemed to know that my workers finished at the normal closing time while I stayed back after they'd gone. But I told him that I hadn't given the matter a second thought.

During the conversation, he spoke about the old house that could be seen from my workshop, and he told me that many people had tried to make their home there, but strange goings-on had put an end to that. The sound of chains jangling outside the house at night along with the sound of a rider galloping by on his powerful black steed, as well as objects moving around inside the house, had made any would-be tenant abandon any idea of living there.

He also told me that an intense blue flame burned on the ground near the barn. As he was a native of the region, he assured me that this meant that there was treasure buried on the site.

I asked him if at any time he had tried to forage around there, but he explained that the owner of the property was a miserly individual, and he preferred to keep his insights to himself. Our conversation finished at that point.

The old house.

Surprisingly, after a few days, another local, David, came by. After introducing himself, he told me that he had something that was going to interest me a lot. He'd brought a leather case around a meter long with him, and on opening the case, I saw a device with an antenna attached to it. I imagined what it was straightaway, and I told him that when he asked me if I knew what it was.

He explained that it was new and hadn't been used before because all the instructions were in English, which didn't present any problem to me.

I started to test it out and found that it was very easy to manage, being small and not very heavy, precise, and apparently very powerful. David had bought it overseas. He indicated also that he knew places in Huasteca Potosina, in a town called Ixtla de Santiago to be precise, where there was treasure buried, but he couldn't go there because his wife was strongly against the idea. They apparently argued often about the subject.

He suggested that I keep the device so that I could use it and offered to introduce me to other locals who were familiar with the sites he was speaking about.

The whole deal had piqued my curiosity to such an extent that I immediately set about making arrangements so that I could visit these places on the weekend. We reached an agreement about the price of the device, and then he left.

Once he'd gone, I started getting used to handling the detector and noticed almost immediately the great precision with which it marked the spot where a few steel rods were. A short while after that, and to my amazement, I turned the television on and began watching a program about a person who by using two spires held in a horizontal position managed to get them to tilt toward the ground and enable the handler to identify the presence of water in arid lands. The commentator explained at the end of the program that several water deposits had been discovered thanks to the clairvoyance of the water diviner.

I had heard of people like that, purportedly with supernatural powers, in the area of Huasteca. It occurred to me then that I should try to contact one of them and see if he could trace water on my property because despite being flanked by rivers, there was a high level of aridity higher up.

The following morning, while I was working, an ice-block salesman by the name of Martin came by. We talked for a while, and he ended up asking me for a job when and if I had too much work for my current employees to handle. I told him I was planning to build a water cistern, which prompted him to tell me that his uncle had the ability to detect vital liquid as well as build wells. I asked him to put me in contact with him.

A day later, at seven in the morning, Martin and his uncle arrived at my workshop. The uncle was a man of advanced age—in fact, he was ninety-four years old—but it was his eyes that attracted my attention more than his age. If you can imagine the eyes of a dead fish, then that was what this man's eyes were like. He seemed unusually calm, and after talking for a while about my plans and interests, the old man took a fork from a tree and started walking around the workshop.

I watched the fork moving in circles in his hands. It was different to what I'd seen on television. He marked three places in a line and assured me that water was present at the rear of the workshop as well as in the center at a depth of seven meters. I believed him and marked the zone and proceeded to pay him for his services.

A man by the name of Mr. Camilo visited me some time after that. He was a cousin of my ex-wife, and I told him what had been happening and that I wanted to be sure that the site where the presence of water had been indicated was marked correctly. After inspecting everything, he told me that I had to place a rock from the river in the exact spot at midnight and pick it up carefully the following morning. If the rock was humid and a drop of water sat on its surface, then we could proceed with the drilling. What seemed odd in the sea of strange things was the idea of placing a rock there at midnight!

I thanked Camilo for his suggestion and continued working. Later that night, I sent one of my helpers to get the rock from the river. All those there studied me with great interest. I had the feeling that they knew something that I didn't.

I returned at daybreak the next morning, anxious to find out what had happened. When I picked the rock up, I could clearly see the dripping water underneath. Camilo joined me later, and we concluded that the old man had done a good job.

In the passing parade of people that seemed to include my place on their list of places to visit in the area, a rancher from the town of San Martin called one day. He was a tall well-built man with a pleasant smile. He asked me if I was the panel beater because he'd been referred to me through other satisfied customers of mine. During our conversation, I told him about the plans I had for the place, including the matter of the water cistern. He seemed impressed and offered to help me.

He asked one of my assistants for a tree fork, which he stripped before walking around the property until the branch started to pull his hands downward toward the ground. He marked the spot that it had indicated straightaway.

Besides indicating the point, he also showed me how to use the tree fork. I asked one of my assistants to try first, but nothing happened when he did; so I took it from him, and almost immediately I felt it make a strong downward movement. In fact, I had little control over it although I could feel my own energy rising at the same time. Based on what was happening, it was clear to see that the old man had picked the right spot in the first place.

Later at home, I started practicing with the detector on the front veranda, all the while being watched by my neighbor, a schoolteacher by the name of Bere. There was little doubt that she knew what the device was for, but I still gave her a brief explanation, which prompted her to ask me if I was planning to look for treasure and if the prospect of that held any fears for me. I assured her that it didn't.

She seemed to know a lot about searching for buried treasure and proceeded to tell me a series of stories, pointing out that many who had sought riches had ended up dead. Her father, it seemed, was one of those who had tried; but in the attempt, he had apparently been deserted by his companions. She told me that her father had rods and spires covered in gold. These "compasses," for wont of another word, could indicate the direction one had to take as well as the very location of the treasure and the depth that it was buried at.

This depth is calculated by the level of energy emitted, but much experience is required before it can be properly calculated.

Thanks to this conversation, I discovered what had happened on the last occasion that her father and six other people, who were not afraid of anything, went on a complicated treasure hunt.

They went to a mountain and started digging, but at midnight at the site where they were camped, they heard the sound of horses galloping toward them along with the sound of carts being pulled behind them at great speed. Mr. Benito, Bere's father, reminded everyone that no matter what happened, they weren't to stop working. A few seconds after that, a strong wind started blowing, along with the sound of chains being dragged across the ground. Then they all saw a black stallion, whose eyes seemed to be on fire, being ridden by a huge rider. Terrified, everyone save Bere's father ran from the scene, and one of those there that night eventually died from the fright that the experience produced. Bere's father, on the other hand, stayed right where he was and even spoke to the mystery rider who informed him that he was the owner of all the buried treasure in the world. On hearing that, Bere's father replied that if that was the case, what was the point of seeking gold that could never be used? The rider, apparently amused, roared with laughter before galloping off into the night.

When the others returned after collecting their things, they found a few pots with nothing more than ashes in them scattered around the site. The rider, my neighbor concluded, had already taken anything of value.

The being that rode that stallion was the very personification of a great evil spirit, a demon of immense power that possesses the gift of being able to transform himself into a figure of terror to mortal beings.

Bere believed that if all those there had not been frightened off, they would have actually discovered treasure, but that was denied them by their own cowardice. I told her that I would like to meet her father and to accompany him on an excavation. She asked me if I was sure that that was what I wanted to do, and I told her that it was.

Time passed, and every time I saw the schoolteacher, I asked her if she'd spoken with her father; and in the end, she informed me that she'd arranged a meeting with him.

Don Benito, a tall thin fair-haired man with a friendly smile received me courteously in his house, and we spoke for two hours about the recent goings-on at my workshop and my handling of the tree fork. When it was his turn, he showed me his rods and how he used them, pointing out that they worked in a counterclockwise direction and that perhaps I would need more powerful ones for my own personal use. He used them in the house while I watched, concentrating on different things that he said could be found under the floorboards but informing me as he continued that he couldn't retrieve anything because he was only renting the house.

We made arrangements to go on a search together, and I told him I would return that night so he could show me where treasure was buried.

At the agreed hour, we left to visit several sites outside the city. He explained that some "burials" couldn't be retrieved because of curses placed on them through black magic. The point of doing that was to stop anyone from ever finding them. The only sites that could be accessed were family lots or those buried by descendants of the original owners. The following night I returned to the places that we had visited to try my metal detector out. It registered the treasure caches immediately with great precision. I was convinced now about the great power of the rods.

I told everybody at the workshop what had happened, which seemed to surprise them. So I asked them if there was something that I should be aware of; and Chano, one of the workers, told me that Don Benito was known in the area as a witch doctor because he was a healer and ran sessions of spiritual cleansing for those who believed in his powers. That explained the certainty with which he had spoken about the sites and his knowledge of them. It was the reason why we had gone there at night.

After listening to what I had said, Chano told me that there was buried treasure in the zone where his father-in-law lived but that nobody had helped him retrieve it for fear of their life. I told him that I wanted to talk with his father-in-law to see if we could use my detector and also to confirm that everything I'd just been told was true.

2

Exploring the Lands of Don Chano

T he next day Chano's father-in-law came to the workshop and told me what he knew about the subject of buried treasure in the area that he'd lived most of his life in. After hearing what he had to say, I couldn't wait to get started, and we agreed to meet the following morning and go to one of the sites to dig.

We went straight to the site and started foraging around, and the detector confirmed the presence of treasure in each of the places checked. I took part of a rock back to the house of Don Benito, who assured me after examining it for five minutes that it was part a large pot, around a meter in diameter, which agreed exactly with the dimensions that the metal director had indicated. The treasure, he added, would be found at a depth of one meter below the surface.

I made the necessary arrangements to start the dig as we had planned, and on arriving at the ranch and expecting the owner to show up brimming with excitement, I got to work on my own straightaway. I had a potion with me that Bere's father had prepared, and I wet it with a neckerchief because I planned to put it over my nose when I opened the pot that contained the treasure if and when we found it. I started scratching around, and while I was doing that, I noticed that the earth was very loose. After half a meter, I started finding pieces of old earthenware and bags of ashes. The soil was a different color as if it had been burnt, and as I progressed, I heard the loud buzzing of bees. The sound of that sent a chill up my spine right away, and I had to stiffen my inner resolve to keep on digging. The buzzing stopped suddenly, right at the moment when Chano's father-in-law arrived. He seemed confused when I told him what had happened because he said he'd heard nothing out of the ordinary when he was approaching other than the sound of my digging.

I had reached a depth around a meter, and the soil had changed color again just before hitting the underlying rock. But there was nothing there.

I used my detector again, but it didn't register anything. I took a sample of the ash, filled the hole in, and took the sample to Don Benito's house, who analyzed it in another room. I had no idea what he was going to make of it, but after a while, he came back out and told me that the owner of the treasure was there when I was digging and that the buzzing of the bees meant that I didn't have approval to retrieve the bounty. For that reason, he explained, the burial site had been changed.

Benito asked me to take him to the spot, and when we got there, he took out the rods and found the new location of the treasure. He told me seven years would have to pass before I could attempt to dig it up again. I respected what he had to say but didn't feel all that convinced just the same. He also mentioned that if I had made the correct petition in the first place, I would have probably finished up with the treasure. I had no idea what he meant by that, and the ensuing silence and the look of confusion on my face prompted him to explain that a petition requires the treasure seeker to speak to the owner spirit so he can ascertain what needs to be left in exchange for the treasure's removal.

He didn't bother to add any more and left it at that.

I went to Mexico City the following weekend to buy material for my workshop and also to visit my family. But my brother Hector wasn't too impressed by what I told him I'd been doing, so as a sort of warning, he told me a story about something that had happened to a family he knew well.

Something strange, he said, had been taking place in a certain room in a house in the area I was in, and the occupants had been unable to sleep. Somebody had told Hector that the reason for that was that treasure was buried under the house, so they'd decided to remove the floorboards and dig up whatever was there. Along with basic rods and detectors that some of them had, they also hired sophisticated equipment that could register precise locations, convinced that they would find extraordinary riches that would more than cover their initial investment. When they finally reached their target under the house, they found a *paila* (an old earthenware pot around eighty centimeters wide) loaded to the brim with treasure, which, after being divided among the four of them, was going to leave them comfortably well-off for the rest of their lives. On lifting the pot out, they found a rag doll, better known as a *fetiche*, underneath. They paid the doll scant attention, so it was thrown away before they divided up the treasure and returned to their homes. But forty days after that, they found four of the diggers dead, their autopsies revealing massive intestinal damage!

After hearing my brother's story, I understood why my activities had concerned him as much as they had, but I assured him that I wasn't going to get involved in anything like that.

I returned to Tamazunchale and sought out Don Benito and told him the story, to which he replied that none of the people would have died if the doll had been placed in a bucket filled with water until it had come apart in pieces and then been buried properly.

They would all be still alive, he repeated, each one of his words underlining my growing interest in the supernatural, my knowledge of which was growing every day.

When I got home, I found Bere waiting for me, and I told her that I wanted to have a look around the old house that could be seen from my workshop. I planned to go at midnight and confirm the story of the night rider at the same time. The idea of me doing that seemed to surprise her because it meant that I wasn't scared about going there alone.

I was getting tired of being asked whether I was frightened about doing things like that. *Why does everyone keep on asking me the same question? Do I look like a coward?*

The following morning I visited her father and brought him up-to-date about what I'd been doing during the night. I told him that I'd searched the old house and that the detector had registered a strong reading in the central yard. But I wanted to reconfirm that with him, so we went back again, and the detector registered the same reading. We checked the surrounding area to make sure that there was nothing that could impede the excavation, and pleased with what we had done, we agreed to meet the following day.

The next morning I started to get all the necessary implements together. I didn't have what I needed to buy very clear when I arrived at the hardware store. Bere's husband, who had been away on a trip, came in not long after I arrived and started talking about his father-in-law. He told me straightaway that he didn't believe in esotericism or appearances but nevertheless respected everything I told him about my experiences up to that point. I told him I was planning to go on a midnight dig that very night and asked him if he wanted to come along, and to my surprise, he said he would.

Our conversation had taken place while the store manager, Jose, was attending other customers on the telephone, so I was confident that he hadn't overheard anything.

3

First Digging at the Old House

At the first light of dawn, I met the cowboy Honorio Villegas. He was passing by with his cattle, and we struck up a conversation, for the most part centered on whether he was interested in joining the little group that I had assembled. I told him that we'd go to the old house around midnight and that Bere's husband was going to come along. That seemed to convince him that we knew what we were doing, so he said he'd join us.

I went with Honorio to the house and once again checked everything out with the detector. This time it registered a strong reading in the inner yard, one meter from the edge of the foundations. That was going to make digging hard because we would have to start outside the building and construct an inclined tunnel. On the other hand, the building was made entirely of adobe, which meant that we weren't going to strike iron rods anywhere.

We agreed to return later, and I went back to the hardware store to speak with Jose. He already knew quite a lot about me from comments he'd heard about the workshop, so I didn't have to explain my reason for purchasing what I wanted. I guess he imagined, based on what I ordered, that I was going to build something; but in the end, I decided to tell him my real reason for buying wedges, ropes, lamps, and the other things I needed. Jose didn't believe in treasure seeking, but the idea of observing something connected to the supernatural intrigued him.

I invited him to my workshop later in the day so he could watch me use the tree fork, which amazed him, and he told me when I was ready to start digging that I could count on him.

I was pleased now that I had three people to help me on what was likely to prove to be a very daring adventure. All that remained now was to buy provisions for several working days because the task was going to take us at least four nights, given the difficult terrain. Now that I had almost everything ready, I went to speak with Don Benito and find out if he was interested in joining the group, but he told me that he'd find a way of helping us out in due course but wouldn't join us for now.

I had my team ready, and the prospect of Don Benito joining in at some future date got me excited, and I felt a brimful of enthusiasm and organized the dig with the others for Monday night.

The silence weighed on us before we started; not even the sound of a cricket could be heard, which was strange for that time of year seeing that the little insects were normally everywhere.

We started working at a steady rhythm until we had made a square just under the flagstone, at the point indicated by the detector and Don Benito's rods. But by that time, the aurora had come up, so we stopped digging for a couple of hours to regain our strength before starting again.

That morning I asked Chano a shrewd question, "Could you sleep with that racket the crickets were making?"

He smiled. "I'm used to it."

We met in the same place under a beautiful moon but once again in inexplicable silence. As we dug, the earth changed color, becoming a mixture of pink and white and emerald green, speckled with river pebbles, objects, and colors that shouldn't have been there. The arduous work of removing them took most of the night.

In trying to make the work easier and to get something to help us against the ever-present obstacles, I decided to buy some new tools.

With the aid of those, we advanced to a depth of three and a half meters, where the earth was burnt and dry and in an extraordinary array of colors. When we had finished that day, I went to see Don Benito, who seemed surprised by my appearance, telling me that I stank of copper, which he said could be countered to some degree by using a neckerchief. The site, he said, could be very dangerous; and he noted that my skin looked yellow, which meant that I wasn't worrying enough about my health. He said he would join us that night.

When he did come, he noted that the whole team looked tired, and he checked each of us over before going down into the depression with his rods to check it out. There seemed to be some discrepancy between the depth that my detector had marked and what Don Benito established with the rods, setting the target at around a depth of one meter.

He looked back up at us with a serious expression on his face. "Regardless of what happens tonight, we stay right here where we are. No one leaves. Have you got that clear?"

Don Benito said it was time to continue. I went down first because I had been given the task of taking the copper lid off. We were already at a depth of five meters, and the pungent smell of copper filled the air. Higher up, there was a strong current of air, which we could see clearly enough when we occasionally turned our heads from our silent labor.

I was deeper than the rest, and Don Benito from above on the edge of the digging was watching the buckets of earth coming up one after the other. Suddenly, those at the top jumped up, the sound of hoofbeats coming from around forty meters from the house sending a chill up their spines. They apparently could see the rider while the rest of us digging could only listen in amazement to what they were telling us from above.

What we did hear, however, was the sound of coins falling from a sack as the light from the lamps went out, and shouts came down through the darkness for us not to lose our nerve. It was reassuring to hear their voices, but I was calm enough because I had expected some sort of problem from the minute we started digging. I yelled back, telling them where the emergency lamps were; and as soon as we could move, Don Benito told us to come up so he could explain what had happened. He'd already put his rods to work, but unfortunately, they registered nothing. They were completely static. We stood there in stunned silence and slowly gathered everything we'd brought, stored it away, and left.

To a certain extent, we were content because the situation could have turned out to be a lot worse than it was. Bere's father told me to go to his house during the day. We rested, and during the morning, I went to the workshop just to let them know that I would be at home if anything came up. I slept ten hours straight; and when I woke up, I went back to the business again, but everybody had already gone. I found a note, though, saying that two important customers would be back the next morning. I went home again, determined this time to stay put and not go out again for any reason.

The next day I went back to work and attended to my customers, and when the workers arrived, I took them to the excavation site so they could fill in the depression we'd created while I went back to work. I hadn't been back there all that long when I saw them returning. It seemed strange to see them come back so soon, and I sensed that something must have happened; and judging by the look in their eyes, I could see I wasn't far from wrong. They told me, in fact, that while the two of them were filling in the hole, they both felt a cold hand pat them on the back. The experience had left its mark, and one of them hardly had a drop of blood in his face from the fright while the other one was calm enough and could even see the funny side of the chilling encounter. I sent them straight home.

An hour later, two workers passed by and asked me for some work, so I took them back to the site to fill in the hole; but this time, I accompanied them until the job was finished. Honorio showed up halfway through the job and helped us out. Then I asked the day workers to leave a part of the debris outside my workshop and to clean the rest of the yard up.

Later, Honorio told me that before I went on any future excavation, a ritual had to be performed in honor of the guardian spirit of the place where the treasure was located. The rite comprised cooking a *patlache* (a *tamal* of five meats that is accompanied by brandy and a *caguama* or large beer). All this has to be done by a medicine man, the rite being spoken in Nahuatl (indigenous language) with the spirit, who would then indicate what else it required if the diggers were to retrieve the treasure. I had no intention of doing any of that but thanked him just the same for his advice, telling him that I would think it over.

I headed for Don Benito's house, and he tried to keep my spirits up despite what had happened the previous night. He'd been provoked by the same devil, so he knew what he was talking about. There were times when the diabolic owner would permit a treasure to be removed and times when it wouldn't. But in last night's incident, my presence had been perceived and the power that I emitted, sensed. That was why nothing else had happened. What he stressed was that if I went there again, I shouldn't be afraid and that if he offered me his hand, I shouldn't accept it, for then I would be lost. I thanked him for his advice and left.

The next day Señor Gonzalez, a truck builder, came to the workshop. He had heard about my search for gold, and I told him in a roundabout sort of way what I was doing. Then he told me that on one occasion while he was building a road, the machinist working for him couldn't remove a rock that was obstructing the track. It wasn't that big and should have been moved easily by the earthmover; but it had proved impossible to budge, and in the end, the attempt to move it damaged the vehicle. Then one of those present there suggested that a "custom" should be carried out. They made a patlache and placed it on the rock, and when the ceremony was over, the driver returned to his vehicle and tried to move the rock again; and amazingly, it was moved aside with the least possible effort, as if there hadn't been a problem in the first place. Once again, it didn't strike me as something that I would want to get involved in because it was, in effect, an offering to the demons.

After this anecdote, Señor Gonzalez told me that he knew a place where there certainly was a large treasure buried because he'd seen a very "high" flame emitted from the spot. If I wanted, he said, one day when I had enough time, we could go and inspect the site. He also indicated that he had some good people he trusted who could help out if required. I asked him to give me a few days to think it over. It was really only a question of making the necessary arrangements.

4

Excavation at Ixtla de Santiago

During the week, a rancher from the town of Tepemiche came to the workshop. He arrived in a damaged Ford van that he wanted repaired because the model was considered a classic. He proposed a deal to me that involved part payment in the form of giving me an automatic Cherokee Jeep. He assured me that the jeep was in perfect mechanical condition, which made the deal seem perfect to me because that type of vehicle was exactly what I needed for expeditions in the interior.

Two or three days later, David, the person who sold me the metal detector, showed up. He'd come to invite me to accompany him to Ixtla to check out the property of an acquaintance. I told him that the weekend might be a good opportunity to do that, which would give me time to give the jeep the once-over and make the necessary adjustments because the roads in the area he wanted to go to were not in good repair.

While I was washing the car at home on Saturday morning, a youth selling health food products dropped in. He offered to help me clean the jeep, and as he watched me working, he told me what good-reputation vehicles like my new purchase have in the surrounding region. I told him that I was hoping my jeep would justify such praise and that I would soon find out. Whether or not he was just trying to sell his products or not, I don't know, but he said he would be able to get customers for my workshop from the people that worked in his company. He seemed like an open, trustworthy young man, so I told him about the purpose of my trip to Ixtla; and when he heard that, he said he wanted to come along because he'd heard about people who had found gold there. It seemed like a good idea. He'd be company along the way; and besides, if anything went wrong, he could probably help me out. We shook hands on a deal that saw him accept whatever I deemed fair as his share of anything we found.

When we picked David up, I introduced him to Jose; and based on their reaction, it seemed that they already knew each other.

On the way, leaving federal territory behind and crossing rough country between the main roads, I gave the jeep a good workout. It was beautiful country to drive through despite the difficult terrain. The multitude of colors and variety of contours were working their magic on my mood the farther we went.

We drove past a very old church, and David told us that there was an enormous cache of treasure buried under the edifice, but no one had ever dared to dig it up and that apparently somewhere in the church there was a door that led to the caves of Xilitla. He also mentioned a cascade in Taman, and we all agreed that we would have a look around on our way back.

After another hour, we arrived at our destination, a small and very picturesque town, where our guide, a cousin of David's, was waiting to receive us in his house.

We ate something, rested a little, and then walked to the mountain slopes. The place was very beautiful but difficult to negotiate because of the humidity and the vegetation there. But we had made it that far and were on a mission.

When we got to the target, I started to get an idea of how much this expedition was going to cost me. In the region of Ixtla, there are scant economic resources; the house that we were staying in was built entirely of lianas without any adobe. Poverty reigned everywhere.

David started relating some stories about the area we were in. He told us that in the nearby terrace, there was only one room because he had demolished everything else because of what had happened there. He explained that he and his wife were having a nap one day when suddenly a flame that reached a height of three meters shot out of the ground. The shock caused his wife to fall off the bed, and she died from fright.

Subsequent to the terrible event, the faith healers of the region told him that what was buried under the house had caused the flame to flare up.

A week after that, and after burying his wife, he tripped over an object; and to his amazement, he saw the side of a pot (strange as it hadn't been there before).

He started pulling at it until it eventually came out. But instead of throwing it away, he took it to the medicine men, who told him that there were three utensils buried on his property that he needed to go back and dig up because the pot had appeared because of his wife's death. He wasn't keen on digging those things up that day, but the following week when he was ready to, he found nothing. He hired a cousin of David's after that to do the digging, and a very old Indian arrow was found, which dissuaded him from looking any further.

The proposal of the owner of the house was that we took out whatever was buried on his property because he didn't want to die before seeing what had been buried there. If we managed to do that, he said he was going to give us half and share the rest with his neighbors. It seemed like more than a fair deal to me; and I said we would return with Don Benito to study the area, but I would give it a quick check over first. The amazing thing was that I found three sites straightaway and told Jose that I would take earth samples from each point and take them back to Bere's father. I packed my detector away, and we left bound for the Taman cascades.

We spoke with the local people about the history of the beautiful waterfalls. One of the indigenous people there noted straightaway that I wasn't from the region and wanted to know what my interest in the area was. I told him that even though I wasn't from the immediate area, I knew the Roque Sánchez well, which was also well known in the zone. Everyone seemed to change their attitude toward me after that.

Our guide told us about the site, explaining that the cascades possessed curing waters and that many came early to bathe in its waters in order to treat chronic pain in their bodies. He also commented that behind the cascade, there was a cave that had been covered up because many people had been trapped in the cavern after entering it, and many of those poor souls had never come out again. The few who had made it back spoke of ancient plumes they had seen, like the ones the Aztecs had used, as well as pieces of gold and precious gems. The strangest thing of all was the neatness that apparently reigned within, as if someone had been given the duty of keeping it in perfect order.

To be allowed out of the cave, black masses were held once a year in honor of the guardian spirit of the treasure. We were also told of other places equally difficult to access and where nobody had ever dared venture. Astonished, and with a lot to think about, we returned to Tamazunchale.

After delivering the earth samples to Don Benito, I waited while he inspected them in another room. And when he did finally come back out, I was not that surprised when he told us that treasure was buried under each one of the three sites there but that the second sample seemed to be the most promising. He told us that we would have to be very careful because great danger existed there. Regarding the pot handle, he calculated it to be very old and that the treasure itself could not be moved for seven years even though the man had paid the extreme price of the death of his wife. The urn had been buried at a depth of six meters.

Once again, he emphasized the danger of the journey and that great care was needed. He said he wouldn't go because he was getting too old for treks as hard as this one was going to be. He told me to carry the potion that he had prepared for me at all times, along with a first aid kit. He added that such an expedition would cost a lot, so I worked harder during the week to make sure that I had every contingency covered financially.

When the day came, I drove to Jose's place, and we went together to Ixtla, where we collected David's cousin and sought the help of some villagers to carry the tools and provisions. When we finally arrived at the house, no one was there, but I wasn't going to let that slow us down. So we started on our own.

We were there forty-eight hours. The first day we found pieces of very old ceramic pots and on the second a moon-shaped rock that was very beautiful but proved extremely difficult to extract. On removing the cover of one of the pots, we found a piece of tree root that had been engraved roughly by a sharp instrument. I stopped to study it and concluded that it was a marker that identified the burial site, so I took it with me.

After removing all the small rocks we found, we came across three egg-shaped rocks. They were very large and as smooth as river rocks but were black in color. We tried to break them up but couldn't. So I covered them with gasoline and wood and tried to blow them up to no avail. They weren't even slightly damaged. We sort of gave up then and left with the intention of giving it another go later, but the tools are still there. We never went back.

On returning home, my mother-in-law called in; and when she saw the small root that I'd brought with me, she recognized it immediately. "Where did you find it?"

"Why?" I asked, intrigued.

"This has been taken from Indian land."

My jaw dropped. How could my mother-in-law have possibly known that? But then, she told me that her father had known about these burials. She knew what the root meant and that there was a great deal of treasure to be found in that place. I told her about the moon-shaped rock and the others that couldn't be moved. She explained that those rocks had been dragged there by mules and asked me if I was afraid of dying because whoever took them out would be condemned to death. Every time I heard that, I took it as some sort of inner challenge, and I repeated to her that I had no fear for my life. But Don Benito had told me the same thing this time, so I decided it was prudent to wait a while before returning to the site. I needed to take my time and think the whole thing through, especially the part about getting those rocks out of the way.

During that week, a person from Ixtla came to my workshop to inform me that the owner of the house wanted us to return because strange things had been going on during the night. A lot of noise had been coming from the excavation site as if someone was still working there. I sent him a message to allay his concern and sent money for him to phone me from the nearest telephone, which he did the following day. He sounded scared, but I reiterated the need for him not to panic because what was happening was a test of his courage (it was the only thing I could think of saying at that moment) and if it happened again to go to the site and ask what he needed to leave there to placate the demons and make sure it was left there.

The next day, apparently, the cries of a person during the night could be heard coming out of the hole, and the owner bravely went out and shouted, "What do you want? If you are going to give me the treasure, say so, and don't bother me any further."

After that, the crying stopped, and I told him to be patient because I needed to check with someone about what the next step would be.

Don Benito told me that all the wailing meant that the owner of the land would have to cry because he would never see the fortune, but I didn't feel like passing that message on to the poor individual (the search for treasure entails great dangers; the devil claims the life of the treasure seeker or one of his loved ones, which is his price for relinquishing a fortune).

5

Excavation of Land That Belonged to the National Army in the Era of the Revolution

D on Alfredo is a well-built fifty-two-year-old from the state of Mexico. In his youth, he was the governor of the state of Hidalgo; his residence then was in the town of Chapulhuacan, Hidalgo, some thirty-five minutes from Tamazunchale. He was working in the hardware products business when I settled in the colony of Buenos Aires and had a branch there.

I bought most of the equipment for my excavations as well as material for the workshop from Don Alfredo's business. It never occurred to me that we would finish up good friends or imagined that he would support my expeditions financially. He was a person who conveyed a lot of confidence, perhaps because of the formality with which he treated all his business dealings. When I greeted him, I always noticed something unusual in his expression. I had the feeling that he analyzed everything—not just his own actions but everything else in the world around him.

One day, keen on satisfying my curiosity, I invited him to dinner at my home; but he declined the offer politely, saying that work precluded him from accepting. The following evening, however, I decided to cook a shellfish seviche and take it to his business so we could eat it together there.

It was a good way to start a great friendship. He invited me to his house in Tamazunchale after that. During dinner, he told me the story of something that had happened in front of his home, which at one time had been a barrack during the revolution and later on a garbage dump before the zone had become residential.

The further into the story he went, the more he seemed to enjoy its telling. On one rainy night, his wife was standing on the rear terrace when she suddenly saw a flame flare up into the night sky. This happened some twenty meters from the back of the house, beside a mango tree. Despite the storm, the radiance continued to flare for a long time before it slowly went out. Excited by what had happened, his wife told Don Alfredo to dig around the area of where the flare had been, convinced there was something there, but her husband said he wasn't going to look for something that he hadn't lost.

What he did note upon examining the site the next morning, however, was that the tall leafy mango tree had withered from one day to the next.

He also confided in me that ten years before moving to Chapulhuacan, on a rainy afternoon, another flame began to flare in his neighbor's backyard. Because of the slope of the land, it flared across to the other side of the street. The person who had witnessed the event formed a group with several neighbors, and they started to examine the site the same night. Hours later, a sudden storm surprised them and forced them to stop digging. They returned early the next morning.

When they returned, they noticed that what they had excavated had broken off on one of its edges in the direction of the street, and in the cavity, a large pot could be clearly seen along with tracks across the earth.

There was no doubt that somebody had been there earlier and taken the contents of the pot. Disappointed, the neighbors had to resign themselves to what had happened and the fact that the treasure had not been for them. One thing that was worth noting was that the pot was a meter away from where they had been looking.

After this extraordinary story, Don Alfredo invited me to his house in the center of the city to attend the birthday of his beautiful daughter, Viviana, the following Saturday. Unfortunately, I couldn't go, which was something that disappointed my new friend because many of his relatives were keen to meet me. I couldn't attend for religious reasons.

When he found out why I couldn't come, he invited me that day instead.

He lived in an immense residential complex, and I discovered that I knew one of his sisters-in-law who lived in the center of the estate.

"Are you the one who is going to die?" she asked me when she saw me.

"Die? How do you figure that?"

She didn't take long to explain. "In case you didn't know, whoever takes what is in those burial sites dies too!"

Her comment surprised me because I'd never really talked too much about the subject with Don Alfredo. I just told her that I wasn't worried about something that had nothing to do with me.

A few minutes later, he arrived. "Have you shown our friend where the treasure is?"

His sister-in-law frowned. "I have no wish whatsoever to die. So I'll leave that task to you."

I said nothing as I followed my friend to the back of the house so he could show me where a fortune was presumably buried.

I told him that I'd fetch the metal detector from the jeep, and when I came back, it didn't take too long to mark the spot. We'd arrived at the moment of determining what the breakup was going to be. He seemed happy enough with the 35 percent I proposed as my share, and I told him I would bring a friend along to help me with the excavation. I emphasized the fact that when and if we hit articles of value, nothing would be removed without him being present.

We shook hands on the deal, and I left to start drawing up a list of what I would need before coming back later.

The following afternoon I went to Don Alfredo's shop for material and found him and a group of relatives sipping beer and chatting.

It was a hot day, and there were worse things that they could be doing. They invited me to have a beer with them, but I settled for a soda instead. They were talking about another in the long line of experiences that had happened to Don Alfredo some years before.

A childhood friend of his had sought him out to invite him to take part in an excavation in a vacant block that nowadays is the property of a friend of his. Apparently, great treasure was buried there after a robbery back in the days of the revolution.

The witness to the burial was a servant who saw a group of men bury deerskin sacks next to a stable wall. Time passed, and it was never recovered; and as a result of family feuding, all those involved in the burying of the treasure were killed in their sleep. The house became the property of the servant because there was no one else to claim it, and over the years, the property was acquired by friends of Don Alfredo.

Six friends who knew the history of the treasure met to discuss digging it up. They shook hands on an agreement that saw them divide the bounty in equal parts. However, when it came time to go ahead with the excavation, the owner of the hardware store noticed that everyone had shown up armed to the hilt; so feigning illness, he excused himself from the proceedings. Whether that was intuition or simply good luck, we'll never know; but in choosing not to go, he saved his life. Almost all of them were killed in a massacre!

One of the survivors said that while they were digging, they heard the snorting of a bull; but looking everywhere around, them they could see nothing. But the snorting continued. Finally, they saw the enormous beast; but when they fired at it, it disappeared, only to reappear a few minutes later, and then disappear again when they opened fire a second time. Not long after that, they discovered bags of gold, and the snorting of the bull started again, although it remained invisible. Then things took a turn for the worse as one of the men, who had reloaded his pistol, started shooting his friends. The survivor fell wounded and played dead but out of the corner of his eye saw the shooter put an extra shot into the heads of all the others.

He was saved from the same gruesome fate because the killer had run out of bullets and took the sacks of treasure and disappeared from the site as quickly as he could. The killer left the town as well, taking his entire family with him. The gold he'd robbed paid for in blood.

The grandfather of the man who had related the story was the owner of some hilly country near the mountains, and before he died, he revealed that near the point where the mountains meet, there was a very old well. When the old man had been a boy, in the time of the revolution, he had seen soldiers storing sacks of gold in the well and sealing the site with rocks that are still there today.

On one of his holidays, the storyteller went looking for the site and found it, but removing the rocks was another matter. Aside from the difficulty of doing that, the whole area was infested with snakes as well as mahuaquites, coralillos, and jabalis. A mahuaquite is an aggressive python that isn't afraid of humans, the bite of a coralillo causes death in less than thirty minutes, and jabalis are wild boars that always move in herds. As if all that wasn't enough, progress through the bush in that rough country is all but impossible without the constant use of a machete.

I suggested that we make arrangements straightaway, but he said he didn't want to go right then because the experience that he'd shared with me in the old house had frightened him. As an alternative, I proposed that I take ten-day workers with me to cut a track through the scrub and carry the equipment that would be needed to extract the rocks. Don Alfredo offered to supply eight well-armed bodyguards, and the man who'd told us the story simply nodded before saying he would give serious thought to our proposal.

"If you're keen on finding gold, why don't you go to the Cerro de la Cruz cave? Everybody knows that there's gold there," one of Alfredo's employees said.

"If there's gold there, why hasn't it already been dug up?" I asked her.

"Just touching it means instant death. Anyone who has tried has suffered that fate. It's an evil fortune. Medicine men go there every year to perform rituals and leave offers to the souls of those who have died there," she explained.

I asked her who could take me to the place because I wanted to find out for myself. Another employee said he could take me to the site but wouldn't enter with me. He seemed intrigued that Flor's words hadn't scared me and wanted to know why. I told him that being alive meant taking risks, and it was all a question of how you handled the odds that made the difference.

I said good-bye and went looking for Don Benito. I told him what we'd been talking about, and he confirmed that everything was true. But before talking any more about the cave, he asked me my date of birth; and after I told him, he went to his room for about thirty minutes. When he came back, he informed me, "If you are brave enough to go, you could enter and leave the place, but touching the treasure is out of the question. That would mean your death."

I didn't buy that and said so, "I don't believe that because I know something that would stop that happening."

He smiled, started for his room again, but stopped. "I don't really know who you are, but to help you enter that place and take what's there, I'll tell you the secret of doing that. There's nothing I would've liked more than to come with you, but I'm getting too old for all this. This is the first secret. Luck is important, but you've still got to follow this plan assiduously if you want to be successful."

I felt privileged that he was prepared to entrust me with a secret that he'd probably kept to himself for years.

"You've got to take a small satchel," he continued. "It's got to be the right size, only big enough to fit one hand in at a time. It should be filled with old coins that look like gold."

I interrupted him, "The only gold coins that fit that description that I've got are twenty-cent copper coins. If they're polished, they'd look close enough to gold."

"Good, that's what you need to fill the satchel with." He paused and looked at me sternly. "When you enter the cave, you can't show any sign of weakness. Stand up straight and announce that you have brought your coins in exchange for his. It would help if you say you like his better than yours."

As far as I know, he has never revealed the secret of the caves to anyone else. I got the feeling that he thought I could get away with it. I thanked him and told him I would bring him his share. He wished me good luck.

I went looking straightaway for the servant who had said that he'd take me there. It was Friday, and we'd agreed to go early Saturday morning. But on arriving at his house, I discovered that he'd had an accident the night before and had a splint on his ankle. I asked him for the addresses of other people who could show me the way; and I went to each of their houses, but they were all too scared to come with me. It was really disappointing, but my adviser tried to smooth things over. "Don't feel too bad. One day you'll go."

But I didn't give up that easily. I went back to see the original storyteller and convinced him to take me to the well. It took me a week to get the right people together: the well-armed guards and the rest of the people I needed to form a good team. But on the day we had agreed to set off, the storyteller had an accident and finished up in bed, unable to move, and we had to call the whole thing off.

When he recovered three weeks later, he was keen to travel. We got the traveling party together again at short notice, assembled the provisions, but he failed to show. The reason this time was a motorcycle accident, which put him in hospital with a fractured foot. It was unbelievable; each new incident in this bizarre sequence of events was making it seem increasingly unlikely that I'd ever get there at all. Was there some sort of curse at work? I felt there was but had no way of proving that. But a ray of light appeared on a dark horizon, at the hospital to be precise. The worker from the hardware store offered me new hope, saying he'd take me there if I wanted him to.

I accepted, of course. I only had to change my clothes and get the coins. While I was doing that, he went back to the hardware store to tell Flor, the other assistant, what he was doing. But when he was saying good-bye to her, she fainted, started having convulsions, and was taken to hospital. We had another incident to add to the astonishing sequence of events that had stopped the trip from taking place. I decided to put the whole thing on hold and forget about ever finding anyone to take me there.

The following morning some more strangers came to the workshop, keen to see and talk to the man with the metal detector who wasn't afraid of the supernatural. My fame, it seemed, was spreading. They asked me to accompany them to a place they knew, but I told them that was impossible for the moment because I had a deal with someone else. But as soon as that commitment was over, I would be happy to join them. We talked for what must have been hours about amazing stories that they were familiar with.

Because of my new projects, I had started paying less attention to my everyday affairs. Fortunately, my business was thriving, and that was due in no small part to the employees I had, who were very responsible and had my complete trust. But I had left my Bible studies fall by the wayside, which prompted a call that week from my family, who were concerned about my recent activities. They warned me about my new direction and asked me to think everything over and make a decision. I knew perfectly well how I should be acting with regard to religious alignment; however, I couldn't give my expeditions up just like that. They had become an important part of my life.

It was strange really that I wanted to get involved in the search for buried treasure, but I suppose it had a lot to do with living in an area like the one we'd chosen to live in. The air was different, the landscape that I saw every day worked on my mood, and I woke up every morning with a spring in my step. Searching for treasure was one expression of a much greater change that had happened to me since we'd bought the house there.

The next day in my workshop, one of my assistants told me that he was the owner of a ranch of around five hectares replete with fruit trees and a small herd of cattle. He asked me to go with him and bring my detector along because at night, in the fields, a violent fight seemed to be taking place. He had gone there several times to investigate the source of all the noise. But he had not only found nothing when he got there, but the racket ceased too.

The fear of the unknown had scared his workers from checking the cattle at night, so an economic problem was being created along with the obvious worry about who or what could be creating such a racket. I went with him that very afternoon, and while we were looking around, I felt as if someone or something was watching us. I didn't say anything to him at the time, and after checking the area with my detector, I found a spot that registered a very strong reading. I told him to be patient and not to let it get to him. I said I would be happy to help him later on.

I went home, and when I arrived, Don Benito's daughter was waiting for me with the news from her father that my new gold-detecting rods would arrive the following week. It was news that cheered me up considerably.

The next morning an old man sought me out at work. He had traveled a long distance with the purpose of inviting me to accompany him to El Cerro de la Campana. He told me that in the time of the revolution, the little-known town of Totolteo in the mountains had a church with a jewel-incrusted silver bell. To ensure that it wasn't stolen, it was hidden on the mountain that bears its name. It can be heard chiming every year even though it can't be seen.

He also told me that a secret way existed that led to a lake at the mountaintop, where great wealth could be found. His son knew these places very well. But people avoided going there out of fear and because they couldn't find their way back. But he had a map that he showed me that marked the way clearly. The plan had been put together by his son, who regrettably had already died. He begged me to accompany him and to retrieve the fortune that was waiting to be found there.

There was no need for him to do that because I was more than happy to go with him. We agreed to meet at dawn at my workshop.

Before that, I spoke with Don Benito, who happened to be passing by, about the authenticity of what the other man had told me. He confirmed it sure enough and added that if I was determined to go, then I should light a torch and burn some of the scrub I passed to ensure my safe return. It had taken the don six days in his youth to find his way out on one occasion; and he'd come back empty-handed—without any treasure and no bell!

I thanked him for his advice and made all the preparations to be ready to go the following morning. But when the agreed time came, my supposed traveling partner failed to show up. I imagined that something had happened to him because it seemed very odd—and even odder when I never heard any more of him. Had he died? Or was his disappearance the work of the devil himself?

The following Saturday I visited my mentor to inform him that we hadn't gone to the mountain bell after all. He smiled when he heard that and said, "I've got a surprise for you."

He had my rods, and without further ado, he invited me to try them out. But I declined, saying that there was no need to do that because I knew they'd work well enough. I planned to try them that very night. He stressed before I left that the night reach of the rods was around five hundred meters. I thanked him once again.

Later, I asked one of my workers to hide a gold bracelet because I wanted to try to locate it with my new instruments. I managed to do that without any problem at all, so I devoted the rest of the night to checking all the points I had previously located with my detector. The rods were easy to work with and very effective. I went back to see Don

Benito and tell him that and to give him a quick demonstration of how well everything was going. We met again at midday the following Monday at his house in El Carmen, and I demonstrated my prowess with the rods to him and his wife once again, marking spots where we should be working.

One day later, Jose and I returned to Don Alfredo's house. To start the excavation, we had to break a concrete slab that the don had placed there. It wasn't easy to split, but in the end, we managed to do it.

It was strenuous digging. Both of us had lost weight despite eating well, and we were in excellent physical condition. But despite that, it took us more than an hour to dig ten centimeters! What was really surprising was that the type of soil we were digging in shouldn't have been anywhere near as hard as it actually was.

At a depth of one meter, the earth changed color, becoming pink and white; and the farther down we went, we started to strike the edges of the mango tree root that we had heard about. The root was completely rotten and dry, and there was no doubt that the reason for that had been contact with shovels. Gas and poison produced by metal had killed the tree.

Those days in that burnt earth were marked by hard work, and we had to set a machine there to provide fresh air because the heat was unbearable the farther down we went.

Meanwhile, the rods were indicating that we were getting closer to our objective. Final victory, however, was not going to be easy, given that we had hit a great slab of rock. In the end, it took us fifteen days to cut through that! And when we did, the stench of copper was overwhelming.

That same day it rained at night, and we were obliged to stop digging. It took four hours to drain the hole. Circumstances required us to place a movable roof over the site in case another storm came. The weather, in effect, had stopped everything, but it did help in loosening and ultimately causing rocks jutting out of the side of the excavation dangerously to collapse into the depression.

When better weather returned, we cleared everything up and started working again. We were around five meters deep, and the color of the earth kept on changing. I put the rods to work, and they indicated a spot in the lateral rock face. I couldn't believe the rods were pointing in that direction. I went back to the surface to double-check, and the rods confirmed the same spot from above. According to legend, treasure can't be buried deeper than six meters. I went back to see Don Benito to get his opinion, and he explained that the bounty had moved, which meant we had to break the rock. It was news that bothered me considerably.

It being the weekend, I traveled to Mexico City; and when I arrived at the estate where I'd used to live before, I met Mr. Muñoz, a neighbor and friend of mine. I told him what I was doing, and seeing that he seemed a little doubtful about what I'd told him, I gave him a little demonstration of the rods' precision. After that, he believed everything I said but advised me just the same to be very careful because the prospect of finding great wealth did strange things to people. But I assured him that the people who were working with me were beyond reproach.

Señor Muñoz mentioned the "capacity" that buried treasure had of changing place. He told me that years before, some friends were digging in a spot that had been checked over with all the right equipment. But during the excavation, the treasure had shifted; and someone told them that to avoid that happening, they had to (according to the secret for immobilizing treasure) to throw lime around. They followed that advice, and it worked well enough.

He also told me that some friends from the state of Hidalgo on a certain occasion had invited him to participate in the retrieval of buried treasure. Because of work, he couldn't go there until his vacation, which made one of his friends impatient; so he traveled to Veracruz, looking for a replacement that could help him. When they discovered the gold, the two individuals who were at the site started to fight over the bounty, and one of them killed the other one and then tried to do the same to Señor Muñoz's friend but couldn't. They both ended up in jail, but my neighbor's friend eventually was released after buying his way out.

I thanked him for being so candid with me and promised him that I would watch my back. After taking care of a few outstanding matters, I returned to Tamazunchale.

6

Excavation of the Hidden
Mines of Tamazunchale

I t was Monday, and I was working when I was interrupted by
new customers. It was a director from the Hospital Coplamar,
accompanied by his beautiful wife. They were both very friendly,
polite people. After examining their van, I told them I could have
it ready the next day. Laura, the doctor's wife, came to collect it at the
agreed time, and we struck up a conversation. She told me there was
something she wanted to talk over with me but said she would prefer
to do that in her house. So following her there, I found out that an
uncle of hers had wanted to search for gold and that he had managed
to locate something through the energy produced by mantras. I had
no idea what mantras were, so I interrupted her to ask.

"There are people who practice meditation, who know how to
open storm doors of energy, which allows them to avoid danger.
The energy of a person who is in a sort of nervous crisis can be

stabilized by this technique that utilizes words that I've never heard before in my life," she informed me before showing me some books that explain the use of mantras. I looked at them briefly but had no intention of taking the matter any further.

To tell the truth, I was confused. I'd come to the house to talk about something that I presumed was serious, and Laura had spent all her time talking about mantras; and to make matters worse, the uncle she was referring to had died after inhaling a strong concentration of gas after the discovery of the last treasure that he had wanted to recover.

She also told me that on one occasion, she had been digging alone at a depth of three meters when she found a copper lid, but her relatives who were there that day had refused to let her dig it up through fear of it causing her death. They put that much pressure on her that she was forced to cover the site up and assure them that she wouldn't try to dig it up again when no one was around.

They sealed the site with a concrete slab thirty-five centimeters thick, which is still there today.

Now after these anecdotes, it seemed that she was getting close to talking about the matter that had caused her to invite me to the house. She told me that she had been watching my activities for some time without finding the right opportunity to introduce herself and speak what was on her mind. She saw me apparently as a fighter, a responsible person, and, above all, a positive thinker. That was why she'd invited me to her house to ask me for a favor.

She wanted us to go to the house of an old woman who lived with her twenty-seven-year-old daughter, Lupe. They lived in the suburb of El Carmen in Tamazunchale and had been having problems with their neighbors because they knew about the existence of a treasure buried in the backyard and were doing everything they could to buy the property.

People she trusted had used satellite equipment to outline on a large scale something buried there, but as no one had reached any agreement to dig it up, some people had begun to take advantage of the fact that the site was occupied by two women living alone. I told Laura I would make the arrangements and let her know when we could visit the women, and three days later, we were ready to go to Lupe's house.

When we arrived, it was clear to see that both women were of humble appearance. They gave me a warm welcome. The younger woman, in particular, was seemingly glad to see a man there. Her mother had told me something about the history of the house, which stood on a steep slope on the foothills of a mountain. Laura told me that the land belonged to her family, who, despite having a good economic position, had never enjoyed the fruits of their wealth. A good part of that wealth, which had been established by her grandparents, had been stolen from the army in the time of the revolution.

Together with a small group of soldiers, her grandfather had buried a large shipment of gold bars in mines and caves and to seal the sites off had dynamited sections of the mountain (after marking the exact position of the gold). In this way, the bounty on the property had been marked. The house had been added at a later date when her grandmother had spent a good portion of most of her days cleaning gold bars on the back veranda of the house before burying them in another site on the same property. When this generation of the family came to its end, Laura's mother always knew where the bars had been cleaned and buried; and sometimes she saw a ghostly white woman come out of a point, cross the yard, and disappear. However, it became that familiar to her that she wasn't afraid. On other occasions, she observed chickens that would appear inexplicably only to suddenly disappear again behind a grapefruit tree. It had been years since anyone had walked freely in the yard because they were all afraid. It had become overgrown and unvisited except for the people who brought the sophisticated equipment to verify reports of the treasure buried there.

After a few years, this corner of the yard seemed more like a jungle than a yard in a suburban house. When I tried to establish the topographic layout of the site, I couldn't because the bush was too thick and was infested with snakes. The old woman of the house kept a squadron of cats as defense, and no snake managed to get as far as the house.

I promised to come back with enough helpers to clear the scrub, and almost a week later, I returned with five laborers. After much effort, we cleared the yard in one day.

The following morning, with the help of my detector and the rods, I detected several sites: one in the very center of the yard beside a grapefruit tree, another nearby, and one inside the house beside the bathroom. As I had detected so many spots, I felt confused, which prompted me to consult Don Benito, who returned with me to double-check my observations, which he duly confirmed.

Later, after Don Benito had left, I went with Laura to Lupe's house. She was pleased with the cleanup work we'd done, and we both agreed that we should enclose the yard to stop the neighbors prying into our affairs.

These costs had to be shared between Laura and me, and the work was carried out by my assistants as soon as we reached an agreement about when to start the excavation.

The next day two young architects in their early thirties came to my workshop. They asked me first for a quote on a small repair that needed to be done to their car; and later, after chatting for a while, one of them asked me about my activities in the search for buried treasure.

I told them about my experiences up to that point, as well as what I was currently doing at Lupe's house; and as was to be expected, they asked me the same old question: "Aren't you afraid of dying?"

I admitted this time that I was worried about what could happen to people working for me; and after listening carefully to everything I said, they invited me to visit the place where they lived, in the town of Chapulhuacanito, thirty-five minutes away.

They mentioned many places in that area and told me some stories about what had happened to people who had wanted to dig up buried treasure. One of those stories was simply unforgettable. It concerned a schoolteacher who always walked home from school a certain way. It was a track that could only be taken on horseback or on foot. It was a difficult mountain track to walk along, but the locals had been using it for years. Often, as the teacher walked along it, she heard the sound of a rattlesnake coming from the edge of the trail; and on one occasion, she decided to investigate the sound and saw a very long snake, around thirty centimeters thick, which disappeared into a hole in the bush. A few days later, she saw the same snake cross the mountain track and reenter the same hole.

Intrigued, she visited a clairvoyant and told him about the snake's conduct. Using his knowledge of black magic and consulting the spirits, the seer told her that there was buried treasure at the spot where the snake had disappeared and that the reptile had been marking it for her. But she could only go alone to that place at midnight, carrying an oil lamp and praying to our Father and repeating seven Ave Marias. Above everything else, she should not be afraid. She had to tell the spirit that possessed the treasure that she would celebrate a mass so that the spirit could rest in peace and that she should take some things of value there as offerings. The clairvoyant also advised her to take a tree fork in case the snake appeared, and if that happened, she would have to hold the front part of the snake down and speak softly to it before cutting its head with a dagger. After that, the snake would separate into two parts, and the spell would be broken.

The next step would be to dig thirty centimeters until she found a sack from which she could take a handful of coins and put them in her bag. It was only in this way that the treasure could remain where it was. After she had done that, a helper could assist her in removing all the treasure.

The architect said that the teacher apparently had the guts to do all that and that now she is the owner of an important ranch. She confirmed the truth of the tale because the clairvoyant is a close friend of her father.

They wished me good luck in my current endeavor and offered me their unconditional support when and if I needed it, adding, however, that the only thing they wouldn't do would be to go to one of my excavations.

After they'd left, I went to see Laura. She was with her husband, and after a little while with them, I got the feeling that something had changed in her. She seemed strange, and I sensed that something was wrong and suspected that the reason behind that could be her husband's jealousy. I didn't say anything and left. But I had the same feeling with my in-laws and even my own wife. I didn't want to get involved in all that, so I preferred to ignore these apparent feelings. I was tired of everyone meddling in my affairs and decided I was better off setting personal goals and working toward achieving those.

The first day that we met again at Lupe's house to work, I was very impressed with the attitude of the two women. They seemed filled with enthusiasm for the project that we had initiated, and that was encouraging.

The harmony of working together was incredible, and the progress that day was a half a meter deep by two and a half wide. That was considerable. We had all the right tools for working. But on the third day, something strange happened, which made the hair on Laura's skin bristle. While we were working, a hummingbird hovered above the site of the diggings. It seemed strange that it would appear there, so close to us, and it was difficult to say what its presence meant.

It came back frequently after its first visit, hovering as always just above us, in the very center of the excavation.

Laura could find no explanation for the bird's behavior, and its presence frightened her; so she cut lianas down from the trees and tied them together to form a triangular-shaped matting, which covered the area where we were working. She was worried that something was going to happen to her or her son who was inside the house.

The next day we began earlier, and this time another hummingbird appeared. These little birds are normally extremely sensitive to human presence, and the question remained as to why they weren't scared away by our movement and the noise we produced. As far as I knew, the hummingbird isn't known for its fearlessness.

That day's work was made more interesting by Lupe discovering a large piece of ceramic inscribed with the letter *M*. We speculated that the *M* might stand for *muerte* (death) or *monedas* (coins). I suggested, however, if we wanted to work at the same rate, we would be better off imagining that the *M* stood for coins.

I brought my recorder from the van and put on some background music to cheer us up while we worked.

As the afternoon passed, I had a small accident with a piece of rock, skewing off a slab I was working on and smashing into my glasses. I took them off after the incident, and only a short while later, we struck a large round rock that had the letter *M* cut into its surface. I couldn't believe that a rock could be marked like that, so I went looking for my glasses to have a better look. And when I did, I found that one of the lenses of my glasses was broken, which seemed strange because it had been intact when I'd placed it on top of my sweater. But the mystery didn't stop there because when I looked closer at the lens that wasn't broken, I saw the letter *M* engraved on the glass!

Lupe's jaw dropped when I showed her that!

"I'll be back in a minute," Laura said, running off.

She came back after a while and said that she'd rung a friend of hers, a clairvoyant, from Ciudad Valles, who told her not to be afraid and that everything would be all right because the engraving presaged good fortune. We finished for the day with that news.

The next day Lupe seemed a little run-down and told us that she hadn't been able to sleep because every so often she'd kicked the blankets off because she'd had a long dream about a grapefruit tree that sprouted yellow balls. She told us this while we were working, and the pungent scent of jasmine filled the air around us, reaching as far as the house itself. It forced us to stop because despite its pleasant aroma, it was overwhelming.

Laura got in touch again with the clairvoyant and explained everything that was happening. The seer explained that the dream had meant that we weren't only going to find coins but gold bars as well and also that there was a special energy emanating from a man who was protecting them. She didn't explain why she couldn't visualize me. In regard to the aroma, it meant the presence of a great fortune, which was accompanied by the hummingbirds.

By now, we had realized how hard the work was for three people and decided that we needed more help if we were going to make steady progress. I rang Joaquin after assuring Laura that he was completely trustworthy.

I invited them to look at the excavation that we'd done at the house of Don Alfredo. Laura was impressed but worried about setting foot on the site and didn't want to go down. When we returned to Lupe's house, the scent of jasmine was stronger than ever, and it was impossible to work. We suspended proceedings till the following day.

I returned to my workshop to see how things were going; and by coincidence, Joaquin arrived at the same time that I did, and I told him everything had been arranged and that he was to accompany me the next day. Just as I finished telling him that, the architects showed up and told me they were going to make a trip to Platón Sánchez, Veracruz, to visit a highly recommended clairvoyant. They invited me to come along, but I thanked them and said it would have to be next time.

Accompanied by Joaquin, I went to Lupe's house early the next morning. I introduced them, and then we went to the diggings. In the first light of day, I was more impressed with how far we'd managed to get with the excavation. It had seemed less the night before.

Laura showed up then, and I introduced her to Joaquin. She seemed pleased with him being there. During the day, we progressed another meter and a half; and by the afternoon, the aroma of jasmine seemed to be less than it had been.

Near the end of the day, my shovel struck something that was very hard indeed, but we decided to leave it for the next day. But as we were leaving, the hummingbirds returned, which struck Joaquin as being very strange.

The following morning Laura didn't come, and even though we could see that Lupe was at home, she hadn't bothered to come across to the site either. So I went over to the house to find out what was going on.

She was in her room, and when she saw me, she wrapped her arms around me and apologized, saying that she didn't feel well enough to continue digging as she had hardly slept during the night. This was worrying news, and I told her to relax and that I'd have a good meal sent over for her to eat.

Joaquin and I continued with the same enthusiasm we'd had the day before, and soon we started uncovering what appeared to be a stone tomb. We were turning up one surprise after another. We kept at it until midnight, and the following morning I went looking for the architects who agreed that it seemed that we had discovered something important where we were working. They also told me that they'd visited a clairvoyant called Doña Nachita, and that she had told them that one of the young people working with us felt sick and needed attending to, and that something unusual was going on where the treasure was buried. They told me that I had to go and see Nachita as I was the head of the excavation work. I told them that in theory I couldn't go because of my religion; but in the end, I went along with the whole group, including Lupe, who as the clairvoyant had indicated was the one feeling unwell.

On arriving at the "surgery," the clairvoyant attended to Lupe first, stabilizing and sweeping her mind clean of bad thoughts; and when she came out, she looked completely different. All the tension had left her face. The same cleansing process was applied to the architect, and when Joaquin went in, the seer started talking at length about a rock in the form of a tomb that would have to be extracted. She said that underneath that, another meter down, a rock the color of jade would be found. At the end of this rock, she said, we would find what we were looking for, but there was a danger to confront because we would have to go through a tunnel that led to two other treasures. This agreed with the history of the house that had been told to us. But just the same, the precision of that woman's visions was truly amazing.

Lupe was then told that she was in love with a very tall dark-skinned man. I knew straightaway that she was talking about me, but I had absolutely no interest in Lupe, which was something the clairvoyant failed to mention.

Returning to the treasure, she indicated that there was plenty to be found on the property. She was willing to help us as much as she could and asked that each time we visited her that we bring a sample of the earth that we had dug up.

That beautiful afternoon we ate tortillas and chicken in a green sauce, all of us together in Doña Nachita's house. The charm of her words had worked wonders on our mood, and a great peace had invaded each one of us there.

The following day Joaquin and I went to Lupe's house to continue working. It was hard going trying to break through the stone that this type of tomb was made of and then carry it away. During the week, we managed to take out all the earth that was underneath it, which meant that the underlying jade-colored rock that Nachita had mentioned was now exposed.

Laura hadn't come to work the whole week, so I went looking for her to find out what was going on; but when I asked her for the real reason that she hadn't come, she seemed evasive. I asked her to be sincere with me, so she told me that on the last day that we had been there she'd noted that her son seemed very serious and that he hadn't wanted to do anything other than sit at the table in silence. He's normally a restless sort of kid, and his attitude that day was puzzling. It worried Laura. Then suddenly the boy spun around, looked at her, and said, "You and that Dominik are going to die together."

The words flew out of his mouth as if he was possessed; his voice and the expression on his face were anything but normal. Laura was taken aback not only by what he said but by the way he'd said it. And that was the real reason that she had stopped coming to the site. She said she could only help out financially until the excavation was finished. I respected her decision, and neither Lupe nor Joaquin made any comment about what had happened. One incident had changed everything and caused her to doubt herself. But that incident had involved her son.

While I was working in my workshop before going to Lupe's house, the architects came again accompanied by their cousin Dr. Rich. The doctor is an easygoing character who became a great friend from then on and offered us his support not only in this excavation but also in the next one. On that occasion, after chatting for a while about the subject of treasure, he asked me to go with him to Chapulhuacanito because he wanted me to check out a point in his house; and as Joaquin had just shown up, we all went together.

On the way, he told us about a river that was dry now but had been a mighty water course not so many years before and that when a man was leading two mules loaded with bags of gold across it, they were carried away by the current. Sometime later, they were able to find one of the dead animals and its valuable load; but the other mule was never found, and he wondered if I would be able to locate it with my rods. I said that I could but that it would have to be at night because the rods' power was much greater then.

When we arrived at our destination, Dr. Rich showed me a chunk of gold obtained from the mines of Valencia, and I passed my rods over that to show him how they work and how to control the pointing of the direction and, when one closes in, how they separate in opposite directions. He noted, as my hands went down toward the gold, how the rods began to turn in an anticlockwise direction and continued to do so after that. There was no doubt that he was impressed by the demonstration.

As I was on the terrace, I shook the rods downward with the aim of leveling their energy; I grabbed them, and they began to mark a vacant wire-fenced block across the street with extraordinary force. It seemed strange; so I stood up, went down, and out into the street, walked in the other direction. The rods began to point toward the center of the property. Then the doctor told me their suspicions about the block because their grandfather had told them that he had seen a group of men bury several sacks of gold in a hole at a depth of one meter; and as well, he had seen a flare on May 3, the day of Santa Cruz, a traditional holiday that is celebrated in Mexico every year. The doctor had tried to buy the property but hadn't been able to.

He took us then to the back of his house, where I checked the yard and found the exact point where the treasure was buried in the place he'd imagined it to be. I suggested that he hire a worker to dig a hole without revealing the true motive for the digging, but before that, he should go and see Doña Nachita. But he didn't want to do that as he wasn't into witchcraft or paying heed to fortune tellers. I advised him to have me present then when he started digging to make sure things progressed well. He had no problems with that, and as it was late, I said good-bye and went home.

The following day we met at Lupe's house and started working because now we had the hard task of splitting the emerald-green rock. We soon discovered that it had the form of a burnt triangular slab, and we needed to use heavy mallets to break it. The work was hard and continued for several days. After cutting through, we found earth again; and after digging another half a meter, we struck an extremely hard rock that was set in the earth at an angle of forty-five degrees. It was emerald green like the other but shone like the scaly back of a giant dragon! It was extraordinary to see something as beautiful as that there but terrifying too. I took a sample of it to the architects, and they were equally impressed. They sent it away for analysis, and the results showed that the color had been produced by the toxic effect of metal under the earth.

While that was happening, Joaquin went to see a clairvoyant friend of his in San Luis Potosi and was surprised to hear the same thing that Nachita had told us we would find there. The only difference being a reference to the danger that we were likely to encounter. This shaman from San Luis Potosi also told Joaquin that a great serpent protected what was buried there, which unnerved my friend to such a degree that he said he wouldn't go down again. It was only after much convincing that I persuaded him to stay with me at the site. I went alone to see Nachita after that.

She seemed pleased to see me, and we spoke for over an hour. I told her that I had everything under control but asked her what I should do in the event of seeing the serpent that she had mentioned. Her advice was straightforward. She said the reptile was very powerful but tame and that when I got close to it I had to kill it by cutting its head open. I would need a tree fork with me to be able to hold it down to do that. She studied the earth sample that I had brought and said that what we were looking for was under the rock that we were trying to split. She reassured me that she saw nothing to stop us retrieving what was there.

I took the opportunity to ask her some more questions about my personal life. She surprised me by informing me that she was aware that I'd had a lot of problems in my marriage for many years and that if it hadn't been for my daughter, I would have probably already been separated. I told her the names of three women that I had known for many years—Patricia Tames, Martha Reyeros, and Angelica Espinoza—and asked her, if I decided to rebuild my life in the future, with which one of those three would I be most likely to have success? She told me that the first two had been hoping I would separate from my wife for many years and that Angelica only saw me as a friend. Nachita noticed, however, that I seemed to be more interested in Angelica, and if something did pass between us, the initial period would be very difficult. But with time, the relationship could lead to marriage. I would be altered by the experience, and my way of thinking would be changed. She added that before any of that could take place, I would have to go through a great adventure, one that involved many dangers. I had no idea what she was referring to, and we didn't speak about the matter again. Before I left, she "cleansed" me and in the process of doing that placed a towel smeared with oil on my head. I left soon afterward.

Driving to Lupe's house the following day, I had the strong feeling that something had changed in me. Only a few months before, a lot of my time had been devoted to reading the Bible, but the previous day I had been cleansed by a clairvoyant; and a few weeks before, I hadn't wanted to enter her consulting room, but now I considered everything she told me to be of the utmost importance.

I decided to think more about this change after work or when I was alone.

When we finally managed to cut through the rock, I invited the architects to come around and have a look at the site. For some reason, one of them started to feel sick after being there a short while, and we decided to go and see Nachita. The seer concluded after listening to what had happened that it had been the energy coming out of the excavation site that had had a bad effect on the architect. She gave the young man one of her cleansing sessions.

Lupe went in then, and Nachita advised her that it was time that she went down into the hole and ask the custodian spirit what was buried there. Lupe never told me what she had to say to the guardian of the treasure, and her silence about the subject is still a mystery to me.

The next day we all showed up at the site when the event was to take place with the idea of standing guard when Lupe went down to ask permission to retrieve the treasure. The key to all hat, according to Nachita, was that no one, except me, could look down into the hole when all that was happening. If anyone did, they were putting their life at risk. At the time, we were at a depth of four and a half meters.

She went down alone, and I waited on the rim of the depression, looking down. She'd drunk a little brandy to help her confront what she was about to do, and once she had reached the bottom, she began her speech to the owner of the treasure. I could hear her words swilling around the hole, the offering of a party to the guardian, and liquor. A voice answered her. It seemed more was required, but on the surface, I couldn't hear what. That voice was grave and hollow, and when our continued presence there had been accepted, Lupe came back up and explained in detail what she had seen through the tunnel. It had been a terrifying scene: a conversation between a frail woman and a supernatural being with an inhuman and cavernous voice.

We started the work again, and almost as soon as we did, we hit a burnt-colored slab. We cut a half a meter out of it, and the strong smell of jasmine came back again along with another indeterminate odor. It seemed like a good time to stop, and the next day I threw gasoline over the area with the intention of setting it alight and burning the gas that presumably lay beneath the rocks. I went through a gallon of gasoline very quickly. We had already taken out all the tools inside the excavation, and when we were ready, I threw a match in. The explosion was that great that we hardly had time to dive out of the way, and the house shook and reeked of gasoline for a long time after. There was no doubt at all that the tunnels that the clairvoyants had been talking about were actually there! It was extraordinary. People came off the street to find out what had happened, and the flame in the diggings took a long time to go out. It was aflame in the center and on the floor of the excavation, as if the burner of an enormous oven had been ignited. It was incredible to watch, and after waiting a couple of hours, we removed all the rocks that had been smashed on the flanks of the site and that could have presented a danger as we proceeded to dig.

The depth now was five meters, and we continued to dig, taking out more green- colored slab until the architects arrived and asked us to stop. Nachita needed to see all of us together, they informed us. We did as they asked and followed them to Platón. When we got there, I went in first, which surprised them because they hadn't seen me go in alone before. Nachita got straight to the point and asked me if I was prepared to speak to the most powerful force of the earth, and I said that I was because I knew exactly who she was talking about.

The altar and, in the middle, Nachita's crystal ball.

When she summoned this being to her fishbowl, it appeared immediately. Nachita could see him in the water, and I could feel his presence. I could feel my skin crawling as she asked him directly what he wanted in return for us to be able to finish the excavation, and he responded that he wanted me. I explained that he knew that that wasn't possible because I was thinking of returning to my religion in the near future. I was then told that what he wanted in exchange for removing the treasure was heads. I then said that he had read my mind when I told him that I couldn't do that because for me he didn't belong to the world of the living, but I said I could offer him a year of service and that I wouldn't say anything to Nachita about what I knew about him.

"Twenty years!" he answered me through Nachita.

I repeated my first offer, and the second time around, that was accepted. The pact consisted of bringing anybody who needed help to Nachita, whether that help be physical or spiritual. Our communication came to an end, and then Nachita performed a cleansing to bring me back from where I'd been.

When it was Lupe's turn, she was advised that she needed to go down again; and then the architects were told that they should assist us, which seemed good advice to me considering the excavation depth that we had already reached. I had built a special staircase even though I usually edged my way down from the sides. On the agreed day, Lupe went down alone, and I was witness to what happened. Although she accepted what the guardian of the treasure said, there was a moment when she paused to reflect on what she was saying; and the guardian became angry, and then Lupe started to have convulsions. It looked very serious, so I scrambled down the staircase as quickly as I could and carried her back up on my shoulders. I have no idea how I was able to bring her up so quickly that way, but I did. The architects threw alcohol on her head.

When we got to the surface, I mumbled some inane comment like "Can we dig?" along with some other equally irrelevant words. I don't remember much at all about what happened then. It was a shocking experience. It had a big effect on all of us. The architects sensed that everything was coming to an end, and from that point on, they gave us constant support. The next day I was the only one who went down to dig. Joaquin had lost his nerve. We had been working for a week, and the rocks were that hard that there had been little progress. But on Friday morning, I went down to clean the site up and took a new pneumatic drill with me that started to cut through the rock easily. The architects weren't there at the time, and when I was about to come up after some very productive work, Joaquin asked me if I wanted him to lower the stairs down. I told him that it wasn't necessary and that I'd come up as I usually did. I always came up with my back pressed against the earth wall because I could see what I was doing better that way and could secure my footing on the exposed rocks. But on this occasion, when I had almost made it to the surface, the rock underneath my feet gave way, and I fell down to the bottom. It was a fall of almost five meters! I tried to fall straight without twisting my body. I was scraped on the arm and the head and took the full impact on my left leg, and despite the high-quality boots I was wearing, I could feel the bones in my leg shift out of place. The pain was that intense that it was impossible for Joaquin to help me come back up even though he is very strong. I asked them to lower the staircase down, and using only the strength of my arms and one leg for footing, I dragged myself up. Lupe took the boot off to reveal enormous swelling. There didn't appear to have been a break, but the pain was unrelenting. She rubbed alcohol over the leg, and taking her blouse off, she ripped it into pieces and bandaged the leg. With difficulty, I stumbled to my car and went to the hospital where I was attended by Laura's husband, who was on duty at the time. When he saw me, he shook his head and asked, "Did this happen at the excavation site?"

I nodded my head.

He took an X-ray and checked that everything was okay. There were no broken bones, but the foot was dislocated, so he placed it in a splint. I went home and stayed there three days without moving around much because of the pain. When I could, I got in my car and went to the workshop, and on one of those occasions, Don Chano happened to be there. He gave me the address of a bonesetter who he said was very good and with a little time would get everything back to normal. I went straightaway to see Don Goyo, the bonesetter-healer. A simple and kind individual, he came down from his house to help me climb the short hill up as it was obvious from the moment I got out of the car that I was struggling. He took the splint off straightaway and asked me if I'd had an X-ray taken. He sent someone to the hospital to get it and studied it when it was delivered to his house.

"That was a great blow that you received," he said, studying the X-ray.

I explained the height from which I'd fallen, and he replied that I'd been very lucky not to have sustained a serious injury. He started to massage the foot, which had no lateral and frontal movement. He massaged it for around thirty minutes, warming the foot and then realigning the bones in the foot. The strange thing was that I could feel the bones resetting themselves and felt absolutely no pain at all. Don Goyo explained that with massages every four days, I would be as good as new in three weeks. What he did for me was incredible because the next day there was no sign of swelling, and my improvement was nothing short of amazing.

In the second week of my recovery, the elders of my religion called me. After a brief chat, I told them what I'd been doing and the experiences I'd had with faith healers, and I accepted my expulsion from the church without much fuss. I was in no doubt about the path I'd chosen. I was completely convinced that I had to finish what I'd started.

A week later, with the help of my crutches, I went to Lupe's house. They were all happy to see me, and I told them after another week's rest I would be ready to begin the final phase of the excavation. Laura told me that because of what had happened, it would be necessary to offer a "custom." I didn't agree with that, but I told them I would think it over before I left.

When I returned to my workshop, Don Benito's son-in-law was there, and he started talking almost straightaway about offering a custom. He said he could recommend a shaman from Rio Claro who would be willing to help us. I accepted his advice and said that I would go and see that person as soon as I could walk properly again. Don Benito himself came over later, and I told him what had taken place at Nachita's house. He asked me how many heads Lucifer wanted. More than two, I told him. He said that that was not a problem and that if I wanted he would bring them around himself. I told him that I would think it over. He also advised me to go ahead with the custom. I thanked him and said that I would do that the following week.

The workshop was the scene of constant visits—the architects, Dr. Rich, and more friends from Chapulhuacanito—and they were all very supportive and prepared to help out with the financing of the custom as well as indicating their willingness to attend. I couldn't believe the support that I was receiving. Once I could move more easily, I went with Joaquin to visit the shaman in Rio Claro. On the way, we picked up a hitchhiker who was carrying a heavy sack; and as strange as it may seem, it was the very person we'd set out to see. Once we'd discovered that, we gave him the money we'd brought to pay for the custom, the preparation of which involved making a tamal or patlache to be eaten on the excavation site and another one to be buried there. The offering would include brandy and beer, pure wax candles, incense, and the utensils that would be used in the ritual.

After reaching an agreement on all that, we went to Lupe's house and informed her that the custom would take place the following day and that other people involved in the search for buried treasure would attend. There would be eleven people there, including Laura, who couldn't believe what was going on.

When the shamans and clairvoyants arrived, we were already assembled beside the cutting. Lupe's mother was there as well after many years of not venturing out into her own backyard. She stayed there until the rite was completed. It was the first time that Dr. Rich had visited the place, and he was obviously astonished. He was impressed by the depth of the excavation and the color of the rocks that had been laid bare. Everyone was amazed at how I could have survived such a fall. As soon as we had exchanged greetings, we proceeded to ask the shaman to proceed with his work.

The shaman and his assistant began to speak to the spirits in the Nahuatl language while we listened in the surrounding circle. We ate the custom and drank a toast with a large glass of brandy, leaving a little in the recipient to be tossed into the hole below. After the ritual with the incense lit, the shaman went down and began to speak with the lookouts. No one dared to peer down, and he buried the brandy on one wall of the excavation site together with the patlache and the candles. Then I was asked to go down. I had no option but to follow the other man down. He explained to me what I had to do to make the site safer and told me what was on one edge and what I would find on the other. But there was no work to be done that day. It would have to wait till the next. It suffices to say the pact had been accepted.

Once the ceremony was over, I thanked everyone for coming, and they all began to leave the site. I took the shamans to their houses.

On the way, one of them spoke to me about an occasion when he was digging with a helper on the mountain where he lives. After opening a large lid buried in the earth, they discovered an immense fortune in gold. The rider appeared then and announced that despite the fact that they worked for him, he would only let them remove the treasure if they delivered fourteen new heads to him. The shaman said that they weren't able to put that number together. This same shaman, who had the power of being able to transform himself into any animal he wanted to be, also advised me that to avoid more supernatural events in Lupe's house, she would have to stop insulting the spirits and also make her own personal custom but with black roosters. If she didn't, he said, she would soon be dead. The explanation he gave me was that Lupe had been afraid to go down and communicate with the spirit and at a given moment had retracted what she had said.

I mentioned then what had happened that day, but the shaman already knew everything there was to know about it. I needed to speak with Lupe as soon as I could.

Back at work again after an interruption of weeks, Joaquin and I dug with renewed energy and managed to make steady progress downward. We came upon the storm door, crafted skillfully from the stone that we'd heard them speak of. But as hard as I tried, I couldn't cut my way through it. I tried my pneumatic drill against it and only succeeded in breaking the half-inch-thick blades as if they were made of wood. I couldn't believe it. I was getting desperate, and looking at Joaquin, I said, "Let's take a sample of this stone to Don Benito and Nachita."

Don Benito asked me to give him three days, and then he would be able to tell me what I wanted to know about the stone. So we continued to Platón Sánchez to receive the not-so-surprising news from Nachita that another custom was required. It would have to be done with Lupe and comprise just the three of us and no one else. She also emphasized that there was a lot of treasure at stake.

On my return in the afternoon, I went to see the shamans, who had the black roosters ready because they'd sensed my arrival. I said nothing about what I'd been doing; and the following morning, when I went to see Don Benito, he told me that the whole affair was becoming far too serious and that it was absolutely necessary to conduct the ritual to avoid anyone losing their life. Besides, I had to deliver two heads; and if I failed to do that, I would have to face the music when the gold was found. I told him I'd think everything he had said over and let him know what I was going to do.

I left, and on the way, I thought that I would never fulfill this deal of delivering two heads because that would be going against my principles. Realizing that meant that I would have to face what was coming as bravely as I could.

The next day Lupe, Joaquin, and I met to discuss the details involved with the custom. The shamans showed up at ten in the morning at a friend's house and brought a stew that we ate. What I didn't know was that the stew had been made with rooster meat. Joaquin ate it easily enough, but Lupe found it hard to eat, and it took me double time to digest it. When we finished, we placed a thin white candle on the plate and were given a spiritual cleansing. Later, we went back to the excavation site, and they started to speak in Nahuatl again and performed the same ritual that they had before. The shaman lit two copal stones—one was the representation of Lupe and the other was mine—but to their surprise, no stone transformed into what it should have.

The shaman went down to the pit but ordered me to follow him. Once he reached the bottom, he began to speak in Nahuatl, and the spirit responded in the same language. He gave me a translation, saying that if someone else came down to help me take the gold up, the spirit would finish the life of the helper straightaway. He repeated his instructions to not worsen the gases at the site, advising me always to show great courage; and if I was going to dig, the architects should be present at the surface. I asked him what he had asked the spirit about the life of the young architects, and he said everything would be all right if I followed all the instructions properly. Then the shaman buried the patlache, more candles, brandy, and beer.

Later, when we had come up, he suggested that we resume digging the next day; but before doing that, Lupe and I had to go to the shaman's house to see what had happened to the rocks he had set alight. He said Joaquin couldn't be present for that. He also asked me for money to get what he needed to use in our presence. I didn't ask him any more about that, preferring to wait and see for myself what he was going to do. I could already feel that this was going to be an emotional day, given the fact that I was going to witness something I had never seen before.

I collected Lupe early the next day; and on the way, she told me that when I left her house the night before, the plate that the candle had been sitting on exploded, breaking in three sections. The only explanation I could think of for that was that everything we'd done up to that point stood for nothing in the mysterious world we were moving in. But I told her I would check it out just the same.

While I was driving, she seemed surprised that it had taken us thirty minutes to drive along the Rio Claro and how far away the shaman's house was. We entered his consulting room, and he invited us into the dining room because one of the traditions of the house was to eat with his family before consulting him about anything. It seemed fairly obvious to me that what we were eating was similar to a custom. He read my thoughts and told me not to worry because the money he had asked me for covered the breakfast we were eating. (It occurred to me then that he was making a bit too much money out of us.) Having breakfast with him there didn't make any sense to me at all, but I needed to go along with everything until I saw what was going to happen with the stones. As well, I wanted to witness to what extent the audacity of our archenemy was going to be and to see at the same time how far I could go. If this ritual was necessary, so be it.

After eating, Lupe went into the consulting room first and witnessed her stone transform into a hummingbird. This indicated to the shaman that everything would be fine for Lupe, but she would have to eat the raw heart of a bird in payment for the offenses that were continually made every night against the king of earthly creatures, better known as Lucifer. Later, Lupe confided in me that she cursed him every night after that. When he asked me to go into the room, my stone took on the form of my extended hand, holding a bar. Underneath my hand was the head of a great serpent. Now I knew why he had always emphasized the point about being brave. That was exactly what I needed to be at that moment. The shaman told me that the serpent would take form in the soil and that I needed to take great care. I was amazed by what I observed and asked him to show my stone to Lupe. When she saw it, her jaw dropped!

On our return, I told her that I wasn't going to eat what he had told me and that I would worry about the consequences. Then she asked me to stop the jeep. The road wound through a thickly forested area, and there was very little traffic. When I stopped, Lupe moved over to me and kissed me, and then we made love right there and then. She told me that she had been holding herself back for a long time, almost since the first day at the beginning of the excavation. She wasn't prepared to go on waiting.

After dropping her off, I went to look for the architects and told them that I was going to need their physical help the following day because it was going to be the last. I explained to them what would happen, and they said that if I didn't want to go through with all that, I should just give the whole idea away. I told them, however, that we were going to finish the job that I'd started, but first I had to go and see Nachita. I thanked them for their offer to take me, but I had personal reasons for making this trip alone.

Nachita was surprised to see me and immediately invited me in. I told her what the shamans had told Lupe to do, and after consulting her crystal ball, she confirmed that Lupe was in great danger. Then I asked her to take me down to El Compadre (Lucifer).

He appeared straightaway, and I said that he could see in my mind what I wanted to say: "Don't interfere in any way with the powers of Nachita because I know that because of your spiritual blindness, there are many things that escape you."

I also told him that I would respect his world if he respected Lupe's life. He answered me through the medium that he would respect her life but wanted me to work for him for twenty years. I rejected that and said that I wanted to speak face-to-face with him. He began to laugh and told Nachita that if he presented himself in his true form, I would fall over the furniture running out of the room.

I assured him that I wouldn't do that, and he vanished. I asked the clairvoyant to call him back again, but there was no response.

I was intrigued as to why he would be afraid of me.

But then, Nachita felt movement in the crystal ball, and a message informed me that he was not afraid of me but didn't want to be bothered anymore.

"I want to speak with you in person," I repeated.

He indicated that I wait for him in my workshop and that he would appear at midnight but that under no condition should I run away. I assured him that I would be there. Nachita told me before I left that she would be waiting to hear what happened and that hopefully everything had worked out well.

Despite my determination not to feel any form of fear, it was hard to avoid stopping the chills that were running up and down my spine as midnight closed in on me as I drove back to the workshop. I sensed that this meeting would determine everything that followed and that my life was on the line along with Lupe's. It was a beautiful night, and as I got out of the car, I felt a strange sensation. "I'm here now. It's time to talk," I said.

I felt a mass of cold air racing through my body. I knew it was him, but I stood my ground as all the tools in my workshop started working. "I'm not here to play games!" I announced firmly.

I waited half an hour for the devil to appear. But nothing happened. I went home, shaking with rage and impotence, not fear. El Compadre had made fun of me.

In the morning I telephoned the architects to tell them we would wait one more day, and then I went back to see Nachita, who had been waiting for me because she could see my arrival in the crystal ball. She congratulated me on the courage that I had displayed the previous night because she had been able to witness all that too. She couldn't explain why Lucifer hadn't appeared because he had on other occasions with other people.

I asked her to connect with him again and ask if he was going to let us dig the gold up. When he appeared, he began to laugh, and I knew he wouldn't let us proceed, so I said, "You are the biggest loser if you don't let us go ahead because there are many people waiting to see results and willing to do whatever is necessary to bring the treasure up." Then he agreed to see me at my workshop the next day. I agreed to that and then left.

In the morning, when I went shopping, I saw that the door to Señora Lucy's house was open. She was a prostitute but also read palms and worked with snails. But beyond that, I didn't know what else she did. I called out to her, and her answer came from one of the rear rooms of the house, "Come in."

She came out of the kitchen only half dressed and welcomed me affectionately with a kiss on the cheek. "Why has it taken you so long to come and visit me here?" she asked.

I was on her list of acquaintances, and she had heard what I'd been doing from everyone else. She said everybody had been talking about me and had given me the name Treasure Seeker, and for that reason, she'd been keen to talk to me. But I asked the first question when I inquired about her work with snails, so she invited me into her consulting room.

"I hope the way I'm dressed doesn't bother you," she said.

"No problem," I replied before giving her a little compliment. "You've got a beautiful body."

We sat down, and after showing me her snails, she said she knew the answer to any question that I could want to ask. "But first, I want you to see what class of person I am," she said.

She grabbed a few snails and threw them onto a board covered with sea sand. They would reveal, apparently, anything I wanted to know. They did that with a series of questions about my personal problems, and then I told her that I wanted to ask her an important question and wanted to know if the snails could respond to anything at all. She nodded and then threw them again, and I told Lucy that my question was mental because I wanted to see how powerful they were. I paused and then asked, "What do I have to do to stop El Compadre making fun of me and attend my call?"

She picked the snails up then and threw them into the sand again. "You have to repeat the following words of invocation: *klim, krisnaya, copisnaya, vallabaya, yaja*, and *govindaya*."

She explained to me that after saying those words, I had to ask the relevant spirit what they required as well form the star of Lucifer, which consisted of six peaks, on the slab of my workshop. I told her I would go and see Nachita and would return later.

When I got to Nachita's house, I told her what Lucy had told me, to which she added that I also had to extend my hand and greet El Compadre even though I couldn't see him because he was present just the same.

That was how I did everything, but Lucifer didn't appear. At dawn, I went to Lucy's house. She explained that after I had left her house, El Compadre had appeared and detailed what he wanted from me. She said that she and I had the same sort of energy and that by harnessing our powers together many things could be achieved. If I wanted to, she was prepared to unite her force to what I was producing. At that moment, she took her clothes off. There was no doubt that she was beautiful, but the thought of having sex with her repulsed me, and I said no as firmly as I could. After I've met El Compadre, I said, maybe things will be different.

My comments offended her, and she said I was the first man who had rejected her. Then she asked me why I had made love to Lupe. I was astonished by the question. Nobody knew what had happened between us. She knew, it seemed, because she had been investigating my affairs with the snails. I felt uncomfortable and apologized and said we should meet again the next day. In the afternoon I visited Nachita, and before I told her about what had happened with Lucy, she said, "I congratulate you for rejecting that woman because if you had gone to bed with her, she would have put a spell on your sperm and cleaned you out of all your money."

I also asked her if she knew about what had happened between Lupe and me, and she said that she did but added that it was just a mad moment and that I wasn't in love with her and she didn't figure anywhere in my future. But she didn't go any deeper into the matter. I wanted to know if she had seen what happened the night before, and she said she had, adding that Lucifer had accepted me as a friend for now. Just imagine that. I was developing a friendship with my worst enemy! The whole idea of that made me wonder if it wasn't some sort of trap.

(Klim kisnaya govindaya copuana vallabaya swaha is a mantra that is used for protection and invocation. Klim, at the moment of being pronounced, causes all energy to be exuded and distributed as a symbol of protection. The krisnaya, gavindaya, copuana operates like a sort of irradiation; and vallbaya, swaha is like the receptor of that protection.)

Five days went by before we started digging again. In that time, people with different types of problems arrived at my workshop. I had to keep my word, so for that reason, I took them to Nachita. I also went to see Lucy again, and she told me that Señor Torres wanted to see me at his home. I told her I would go when I had enough time, but that was really just an excuse. I didn't know anything about Torres, and I wasn't that keen on making his acquaintance. It never occurred to me then that we would finish up being great friends. At that time, my mind was completely focused on what I was doing. One morning a flashy van that I'd worked on previously arrived at my workshop. It was driven on this occasion by the owner, not the chauffeur. Don Torres Perez was an easygoing man in his early forties and wasted no time in getting straight to the point. "How much will you charge me to run your instruments over the ranch and a house in the town of Los Aguacates?"

I was equally direct when I told him, "Nothing."

"If you help me with the digging, what percentage of the treasure would you want?"

"Thirty percent," I informed him.

He nodded. "I'll give you 45 percent. I want you to be honest with me."

"That sounds good, but I can't go anywhere at the moment. I've got too much on my plate. I'm finishing an excavation in El Carmen. When that's over, I'll come to your place."

He seemed to be happy with that and handed me a card with his telephone number on it. "If you need anything beforehand, don't hesitate to call me."

Increasing my offer had impressed me as had the reference to being honest. I liked the guy.

The time had finally come, and with Joaquin, I met the architects early at Lupe's house to finish what we'd started. We were all happy about the prospect of that; but at the same time, everybody was worried about me because if anything happened, no one could go down to help me.

They wanted to tie me from the belt just in case something went wrong, but I told them not to worry because I wasn't going to let them down. When I went down, the rock broke with incredible ease, and I saw a beautiful hollow open up before me. It was a sign that everything was going to finish well. I finished taking the rock out and found sand beyond that. I filled the buckets so they could lift them from above; and that was when, to the surprise of the architects, the hummingbirds came back along with the strong aroma of jasmine (which meant the imminent presence of the owner of the treasure). We continued working. I removed more sand and in the end discovered the first gold bar sticking out of the upper part of the cutting. Everybody could see it from above as powerful lights illuminated the site. I began to push the bar upward with considerable force, and as it started to break free, it was suddenly dragged down violently in the opposite direction as the sound of strident laughter swept out of the earth. Everyone there went pale on hearing that laugh, but fury overtook me as well. "Keep your beggar's gold. Everything's over!"

As soon as I'd said that, the spotlights that illuminated the site exploded, and I could feel the fear of those on the surface. I climbed out, and we all left the scene as quickly as we could. No one was capable of saying a single word about what had just taken place, and despite the fear and shock that the incident had produced, something else was patently clear: even though there was gold on the site, all we could apparently do was view it.

"It doesn't matter how much money we've put into this project," someone in the car said. "The important thing is that we're all still in one piece."

That may have been true, but what was certain was that all my companions were shaking and in fear of their lives and those of their loved ones. The question that kept circling the minds of everyone there was whether there was any point in continuing to challenge the devil. I was disappointed for them and furious with El Compadre, who just had another great laugh at our expense. But what could I do? The sense of impotence and desperation was overwhelming. Even though no one said anything, it was clear that we had decided to give it away, and that bothered me so much that I went back to the excavation site and threw as much garbage into the hole that I could lay my hands before I went home. I let my intentions be known when I screamed into the cutting that I would be filling the whole site in. But while I was yelling that warning, I was also telling myself that I would go down again and confront El Compadre because there was nothing fair about what had just happened.

On the way home, I saw Lucy, and I asked her if she knew of any other effective way of meeting El Compadre. She told me that I needed to consult a Ouija board; be dressed totally in black; take a candle of the same color with me, one that would burn for two days; and make the invocation on a Tuesday at midnight. That was how the following experience began, one that was more diabolical and terrible than anything else that had occurred up until now.

7

Don Torres Perez, the Rancher, Enters Our Lives

I had never been more determined than I was at that moment to speak to El Compadre. Everything that had happened had me fuming. I didn't have sufficient funds to settle the expenses that were coming up for the purchase of a Ouija board or the appropriate clothing to present myself at midnight in my workshop, so for that reason, I told Joaquin that it was time to visit Señor Torres because he had said that he was prepared to help out in any way he could. Joaquin doubted that, however, because he knew that wealthy people were usually less committed when the moment came to put their words to the test. Either way, I visited him for the first time, where I was received with great fanfare.

He ordered his staff to prepare lunch, and during our chat, I told him what had happened at Lupe's house. He seemed surprised by that even though there was no doubt that he believed me because he himself had seen all sorts of supernatural phenomena. I also told him about Lucy. He knew her, he said, and asked me if I had slept with her. I said that there was no doubt that she was beautiful, but I wasn't attracted to her. And I told him about what happened between us, about her being offended. But the incident hadn't stopped us getting on well with each other. Don Torres seemed even more surprised by that and picked up his telephone and dialed Lucy's number and asked her, "Hi, old girl, did you have a good time with Dominik?"

"Don't talk to me about him. I think he's gay," she answered.

But Torres went on, "They told me that you've been seen together with him."

"That's true, but there's nothing between us. He's got his mind on someone else."

They spoke for a while, and then we resumed our conversation. He told me that he'd consulted Lucy on other occasions. I confided in him that she had told me how to contact El Compadre but that I wasn't in an economic position to go ahead with that at the moment. Then he asked me how much I needed.

"I need enough for gasoline, clothes, candles, and a Ouija board," I answered.

All that came to around 800 pesos, and Torres wrote me a check for two thousand. "I'll give you more than you need because I don't want you to tell me that you're still short. What's left over you can put against future expenses."

This man was to become one of my most reliable financial backers in the months that followed. After lunch, I went back and looked for Joaquin, who was amazed at the rancher's generosity.

We left for Ciudad Valles, which was a two-hour drive via the federal highway, and went to a business called Chedraui and bought everything we needed, with the exception of the candles. There were people there from Tamazunchale who knew me when we entered although I was unaware of that at the time. Later, we went looking for the candles in the city; and after searching for more than an hour, we eventually found what we were looking for. The following day we cleaned the workshop because I wanted to have it ready for that night when I would be alone. Joaquin wished me luck before he left.

When I arrived home, my wife rebuked me for my visit to Valles because the news of my trip had made its way back to her. To be frank,

I wasn't worried about that because there was nothing in the world that was going to stop me from going ahead with what I had planned.

When night fell, I left for the workshop and made the invocation at the stroke of midnight in accordance with what Lucy had instructed me. I lit the candle and tried to use the Ouija board, but nothing happened. What seemed odd was that the candle that should have lasted the whole night had burned all its wax in an hour, the exact time I waited for El Compadre.

In the morning I lit a small log in the workshop and threw it at the Ouija board to give vent to my fury after a wasted night. Just after I did that, there were three large explosions. Don Torres was making his way to my workshop and heard one of them. When he got to the workshop, he asked me what was going on, and I told him what had happened the night before. He just shrugged his shoulders and said that I shouldn't pay too much attention to that and that he was on his way to see a shaman that he knew in Tanquián and his advice had always been good. He was going to tell him everything that had happened, and he would let me know later what the shaman advised.

I went to see Lucy, and she told me that she had tried to teleport herself the night before to be with me but for some reason hadn't been able to. She was surprised when I told her about the fast-burning candle, which prompted her to throw more snails into the sand to establish the significance of what had happened. The news wasn't good: my death had been previewed. Obviously, she wasn't expecting a result like that; and concerned, she told me to give everything away and not seek any more contact with El Compadre.

"That's not my style," I told her flatly.

I went to see Nachita, who said that she was aware of everything that had happened and not to worry about telling her what Lucy had said because she already knew. She added that El Compadre was very angry with me for throwing garbage into the cutting on Lupe's property. She said that I had to clean all that up because it wasn't helping my chances of communicating with him.

I followed her advice and went the next day to clean the site up, but the place reeked of pestilence because a dog had died in the pit. I staggered out on the verge of vomiting.

After finishing, I went home; and on the way, Don Torres rang me on my cell phone. He invited me to his house because he wanted to introduce me to a woman, so I changed direction and headed there and was surprised to see a tall fair-haired chauffeur waiting outside Torres's house. White smoke was coming out of the windows because the house was being cleaned. The woman came out coughing, and I took the opportunity to introduce myself. She was a twenty-eight-year-old called Margarita, who, after introducing herself, complained that she was certain to get a headache because of the cleaning agents being used inside.

Torres followed her out a little later, and we waited in the fresh air for a while to let everything get back to normal in the house. An hour later, Torres ordered a pizza, and we continued our chat comfortably seated inside. I discovered soon enough that Margarita was deeply involved in esotericism besides reading tarot cards and using the pendulum. She told me that she'd heard about me, and afterward, I asked her if she could summon El Compadre. That too it seemed was in her power. A ritual was involved, she explained, and the whole thing was not to be taken lightly. She invited me to her house adjoining the federal highway on the outskirts of Tamazunchale, a fifteen-minute drive away.

I decided to find out more about Margarita, and not everything I was told was all that good. I found out that she had a ranch, was divorced, and had two children. I told Torres that I had my doubts about the young woman, but he assured me that she was good at what she did and was willing to help us without payment. That struck me as even stranger because the effort of trying to unearth a treasure was not exactly light work; in fact, many had died in the attempt. I asked him to give me a couple of weeks to get to know her a bit better before I agreed to accept her help.

The first day that I entered her consulting room, I was extremely impressed by the array of objects that she had accumulated on her altar. There was a Christ, some ram horns, a dagger, a Buddha, a great dragon, a square box with inscriptions on it that referred to zodiac signs, and a wall full of a variety of candles (and burners in the form of women, or at least they seemed like that, or virgins, but not from the church). On one of the other walls, there were a lot of potions and four types of tarot cards, including Spanish and Egyptian cards. Some objects were referred to as things of God while others were there exclusively to deal with Lucifer. To see all that for the first time was overwhelming.

"I'd like you to see who I am in your cards," I asked her after finishing looking around the room.

She saw all my personal problems straightaway.

"Sometimes you have had to sleep in the living room. Your wife has a bad temper, and that has caused you a lot of problems. You don't have much in common with her."

She asked me why I had put up with that for so long, and I answered that I didn't want to leave my daughter. I told her about other women I knew who perhaps had a place in my future. I didn't mention names and asked her opinion.

"First of all, you don't drink or smoke, and you're not a womanizer, and that package is not something that El Compadre likes, especially when it comes to digging up buried treasure. He wants you to change. And with regard to the women, one is tall and fair and has problems with colic and a genital problem. She likes you a lot and will ring you in the next few days."

I reflected on the fact that the only person who had my telephone number was Angelica. She also told me that if I had any hopes of her becoming my wife, then I would have to be very patient, and my life during the wait would be very difficult. For the moment, this woman couldn't see the upside in any future relationship with me. I told her then that her name was Angelica before she continued, "I have female friends who would be attracted to the qualities you have. My sister, for one, would fall for you in a big way."

I told her that all that sounded good but that I didn't know any of those people. She also told me that I had been thinking about Angelica for a long time.

She said as well that she could see nobility in my soul and that this also represented a problem in a potential visit with El Compadre. But I told her that it was imperative that I meet him and that I was prepared to go through any ritual that was necessary to ensure that it took place. She took another look at the cards and said that my problem could be resolved, but she saw problems with Torres because it would be very hard to get him to take part in the ceremony. I promised to speak with him and ensure that there wouldn't be any problems.

Margarita explained to me then that I had to mark all the points on the ranch and in the house at Los Aguacates. Then she asked me if I was carrying the rods with me, and I told her they were in the jeep, so she asked me to go and get them. We went to the backyard of her house; and as we were making our way down to a spot that she wanted me to check out, we bumped into the servant of the house, a beautiful young woman, with fine features and clear skin, with the face of an angel. Margarita sensed immediately that the girl had caught my eye.

"She's single and twenty-five years old," she told me.

"She's extraordinarily beautiful," I observed. "But I'm ten years older than her."

She didn't say anything about that, and we continued on to the site we were looking for. The rods confirmed that there was something big buried underneath.

"You're going to need at least one head for what's under there."

I have no idea why I said that, but it brought a response from her. "Of course, that's exactly what I need, and I've got one."

I noticed the expression on her face change immediately; there was no doubt she had someone in mind. What also occurred to me then was that according to what I'd found out about digging treasure up, people associated with witchery couldn't be involved, at least not on their own. It had to be done through other people.

After we'd inspected the site, I attempted to say good-bye, but she would have none of it and insisted on me going back into the house so that the maid could cook dinner for us. The three of us sat down at the table together, and almost as soon as we had, some clients of Margarita's appeared. She told us to start eating without her. I complimented Elvira on her cooking while we were eating. The stew was exquisite, but I couldn't pry a word out of her in response. She seemed very shy, but despite not saying anything, she edged closer to me at the table with a tender look in her eyes. It had been a long time since I'd seen such a passionate look directed toward me. I felt touched by her physical presence and her nature, but it wasn't the moment to take it any further. I wasn't looking for any new commitments right then. I left the house with mixed emotions.

I went looking for Torres and told him what had happened at Margarita's place without telling him about the intimate meal I'd shared with Elvira. We made arrangements to go back to the ranch and take photos of all the spots that needed marking. I told him what the ritual involved, which obviously got him thinking because he said that an event of that magnitude could compromise our relationship with El Compadre for all time. I explained that she was trusted by the Saint of Death, for which reason the offering she would make would be aimed at Lucifer, and that it would be done in such a way that we would be able to unearth the treasure we were seeking. Torres told me that he wasn't having second thoughts because of the costs, but he still wanted to think it over.

We went to the house at Los Aguacates and found a single site that registered a high reading. I told my friend about Nachita, and he said he would go and see her. We went to our respective homes to have a bath and agreed to meet later to go to Platón Sánchez.

He picked me up an hour later. He wanted to know if I had spoken previously about him to Nachita, and I said that I hadn't. When we arrived there, the missus was in the yard, feeding the hens. She didn't seem surprised to see me and greeted Torres warmly, and I told her that he wanted to speak alone with her. After hearing that, she invited him into her consulting room, where no doubt Torres would have been impressed with her altar with its large image of Christ, other religious icons, the crystal ball, and candles. Torres told me later that after he entered, Nachita gave him the sign of the cross before asking him what she could do for him. To which he asked her why I had lost control of the gold bar when I had my hands on it at Lupe's place. Had it been too heavy for me, or was there some other reason?

She told Torres, "What there was at that moment was a power way beyond his comprehension. He could only touch and look at it, and even that surprises me, as does his bravery in actually being there in the first place."

El Compadre appeared then and told her that he will see Dominik personally in due course. She turned away from the crystal ball and looked at Torres again. "What I see here is that you are divorced with one child and that this has caused you to suffer from an illness. I can also see that it was your unfaithfulness that caused the divorce. You remarried, but your ex-wife has tried to kill you. With your present wife, you have two sons, and things are not going that well. You also have a difficult relationship with your father, to such a degree that you don't want anything to do with the inheritance that he is going to leave you."

He started to cry when he heard that because he had never spoken with anyone about the matter, not even with me. She also told him that she would help him as much as she could in the excavation at his house in Los Aguacates, which she realized was about to get underway. He told Nachita that I would keep her informed about anything that happened there. After he came out, it was my turn to go in, and she told me straightaway, "Despite the personal power that this man has, he will be honest in his dealings with you."

She told me as well that I should support him at all times because problems were not that far away. I thanked her for her help, and then we left. On the way home, Torres told me that we would be lifelong friends if we managed to keep our secrets. He didn't want me mentioning anything about his life to anyone else. I assured him that he had nothing to worry about in that respect. Then we went to dinner at Huejutla.

On leaving my home the following day, I saw his van in front of Lucy's house, which I thought was strange. I waited for him to come out, and later, I went to see her. She warned me that if we did the ritual that Margarita had proposed, one of us was going to die. I thanked her for that information but didn't believe it either, so later that day, I went with Joaquin to Nachita's house.

On the way, in the mountains, my cell phone rang; and much to my surprise, it was Angelica. I remembered immediately that Margarita had foreseen the call. I told her about what I had been doing and the different people I had met, about the search for buried treasure, and told her that when I had made a success of that, I would start a business with her. She sounded very excited at the prospect of that, but then suddenly the line went dead. The credit on my card had expired!

We continued to Nachita's house, and the first thing I told her about when we arrived was the call from Angelica. She seemed pleased for me and assured me that we would get along well in the future, but there would be inevitable teething problems in the relationship. She also told me that she was living or would live with a male friend but that there were no sexual relations between them and that this person had gained access to the apartment through black magic. I asked her to annul that magic and remove the person as soon as she could. That was the first favor I'd asked of her special powers.

And being the first time I'd done that, I made a mental note to go over it after leaving her house. There had been a series of stages in my growing belief in esotericism, and that was more than evident in the decision to ask for a favor like that from a clairvoyant.

Then I told her what had happened with Lucy, and she told me that she was only interested in Torres's money but agreed that one of the two would die if the ritual was carried out. I wanted to know what the reason for that was given the fact that neither of us were afraid of going through with it.

"It would be a heart-related problem," she answered.

"Then it couldn't be me," I told her before she looked into her crystal ball again.

She concluded it would be Torres who would succumb. I asked her what should be done then, and she explained that I should do the ritual first only with Margarita, at a crossroads or at Torres's ranch where the two rivers met. I had to speak with El Compadre urgently. I said that I would make the arrangements with Margarita. Nothing was said in regard to Angelica, so I said good-bye and left.

Don Torres came around to the workshop the next morning to tell me that he had no commitments on Friday, which left us a long weekend free to make a three-day trip to visit a clairvoyant in Ciudad Victoria. The person in question had considerable powers, according to Torres, and many artists from the United States crossed the border to see her. She used a pendulum and limited herself to white magic. I confirmed my willingness to accompany him, and after he left, Margarita appeared. I was surprised that she'd come to see me instead of waiting for me to visit her. I asked her straightaway if she was prepared to do the ritual with only the two of us. She took her cards out and looked at them and told me that she would. I didn't tell her anything about the trip I'd just planned to do with Torres, but I think she already knew about that. I told her that I would talk with Torres about doing the ritual on his ranch and that I would come around to collect her when everything was ready.

Later that day, I saw Torres, and he told me that Margarita had passed by to explain the purpose of using his ranch. He said that we could use it but for the shortest time possible because buyers were visiting the ranch in the next few days to buy cattle, and they stayed in a small house that he used to put them up in when they came to his ranch. That house was the exact location of the planned ritual.

He told me then that Margarita would come to my workshop around eleven the following night. I asked him what would happen if in one of the rituals we all happened to be together when El Compadre appeared.

He just smiled. "If that happens, we're all fucked."

His answer reflected the desire that he had to communicate with him. I finished the soda that he had offered me and went back to the workshop to get everything in order for Margarita's arrival. She arrived punctually the next day, and we went to the ranch together. Margarita's driver helped us take everything out, and then we told him to park the car a ten-minute drive away and wait half an hour before coming back for us. I remembered that Margarita had seen her own death approaching in the cards; but I was also sure that now that I was with her, that possibility had been put on hold, at least for the foreseeable future.

Once we were alone, we used silver powder to make a six-pointed star. We lit two black altar candles; and at the stroke of midnight, we both stripped naked (she hadn't explained that before, but I followed her orders without question now). We held hands in the dark, and she asked me to close my eyes. And when the prayer was about to end, I held on to her tightly because under no circumstances could I leave the triangle. I asked her how I would know when the invocation had come to an end, and she said, "You will know!"

That was the truth because even with my eyes closed, I began to distinguish a bright light pointing toward my hands. When I released my grip on her, all our hands were aflame; but amazingly, there was no sensation of being burned. We looked around for any indication of his presence, and in that moment, a great current of air put the fire on our extremities out even though the altar candles continued to burn.

"He's not going to come," she said after calling him.

"Why not?"

She didn't know how to answer me, but I could see easily enough that she was nervous. I decided to take the matter into my own hands. "Let me invoke him, and you can give me the answer to my question through the cards."

I asked her to put her clothes on, and I did the same. And then I suggested that she withdraw to a certain point to give me a chance to invoke El Compadre in my own way because I was sure that he was going to respond to me. She wanted to know the reason for my assurance, and I told her that that was one of my secrets. She left then, and I began to call him internally, calling all his names. "I don't need the complexity of prayers to call you because I know that you are listening to me, and if you don't appear, it is because of what I know about you. I am asking you a favor: if you must take Margarita's life, do not do that yet. Leave her alone because she is a connection for many people who want to unearth the riches of the earth. The last word is yours when it comes to those who want to uncover treasure. I will support the ideas of those who work for you and will reveal nothing about your way of doing things. Please, answer me now through this woman."

After I had finished speaking, I walked over to Margarita and told her to light the lantern, throw the cards, and ask for an answer to my question.

"I see a long life for me," she said, a tone of surprise in her voice as she smiled and looked at me, or rather looked through me. Apparently, she saw El Compadre standing behind me. I couldn't follow what was going on, but the obvious look of contentment on her face was puzzling. She walked over to me and embraced me and kissed me before thanking me. It was all very confusing. (It should be mentioned here that the price for saving her life was very high because her mother had died, and I was almost sure that it hadn't been a natural death. The circumstances had been suspicious, and the authorities had not been convinced that she had fallen down the stairs accidentally.) This strange episode came to an end then as the driver came back from his exile.

Very early the next morning, Don Torres came to the workshop to find out what had happened. I told him everything as it had occurred, and he advised me that the trip to Victoria would be postponed to the following week because the woman we were going to visit was on a trip herself for three days. Before he left, he gave me some money, which he obviously knew I was in need of.

Thirty minutes later, Joaquin arrived with the news that he was short of money too. I gave him what he needed for expenses. He asked me if I'd heard about the robbery at Las Montes Jewelers in Tamazunchale, and after telling him that I hadn't, he told me that there was a reward on offer for information that could lead to the recovery of the jewelry. It seemed a good idea to take the owners to visit Nachita. We spoke with them that night and explained that we knew a person who through her powers could most probably tell them who had stolen the jewelry, which would, in turn, lead to its recovery.

I told them I would only charge two thousand of the 50,000 pesos on offer as reward because that was what I needed to travel. The jeweler said that if the person I was referring to could convince him she knew everything about the robbery, then he would give me the cash straightaway. I gave him my address, and we agreed to meet at ten the next morning; but much to my surprise, they showed up at seven! And that wasn't the only surprise because Lucy was in the car with them. I had no idea that the Monteses even knew her. We all headed off to Platón Sánchez together.

When we arrived, I introduced them to Nachita then left them alone. Afterward, Lucy went in, and Nachita recognized her immediately; and after a few minutes with carefully selected words, she managed to put Lucy in her place.

While we were sitting in the yard, Mr. Montes told me that after dropping me off at the workshop, he would go back to Tamazunchale for my fee money.

That was good news prior to having the last turn in the consulting room.

"I'll come back another day and tell you what happened at Torres's ranch," I said after I went in.

"That's fine, but I already know what took place. I saw the whole thing in my crystal ball. El Compadre was there among the trees, but he didn't get too close because the chauffeur didn't withdraw to the spot that you had suggested. He parked the van three miles away but walked back, carrying a pair of powerful binoculars. If El Compadre had chosen to appear at that moment, the young driver would have perished instantly."

All this was really news to me. I was shocked by what she had to say. I left then to go back with the others.

On the way, the jewelers didn't say anything about the robbery; and when we passed through Huejutla, they invited us to have lunch.

They were very friendly with us. Lucy asked me how long I'd known Nachita, and I told her just a few months. She told me that she was very good and held me in high esteem.

They dropped me off at the workshop at four in the afternoon, and Montes returned to the city on his motorbike to fetch the money.

Some days later, Lucy came to the workshop around midday. At that time of the day, I normally have a lot of customers, but that didn't seem to bother her. She walked straight up to me and kissed me warmly on the face and held my hands. "I need to talk to you. I've got a proposal that I think you'll find interesting. I'll wait for you at my place. Come after your customers have gone."

I nodded. "Okay, I'll be there."

A couple of my customers seemed surprised by the warmth shown by my visitor, and one said, "We thought you were a serious character, but it seems you've got your well-kept secrets."

"She's just a friend," I told them. "It's better to keep things that way."

After they left, I went to Lucy's place. I was surprised by her appearance when I arrived; she was well dressed and wearing makeup. She looked beautiful, and the house was wonderfully decorated with candles. She asked me to sit down at the table because she'd prepared a stew for me. There was wine too, and we ate together. The only time I could remember being received in a similar fashion was by a friend in Mexico City. I have never been welcomed to my own home like that. After eating and chatting for a while, she cleared the table and walked over to me. There were no thoughts of rejecting her this time if she wanted to go to bed, but she only put her hand on my shoulder. "It's time to talk business. Let's go to my consulting room."

That sounded like a good idea. She told me that she had discovered a well with treasure in it, but despite her best efforts, she couldn't remove it. That was why she'd invited me to her house. She explained that there was no money there or bars of gold. There was only a double-sized shoe box that contained valuable antique jewelry. She'd been able to see everything when she had succeeded in astral traveling to the site and later had gone physically to the spot to confirm what she already knew to be true. The owners of the property were also aware of the jewelry's presence there.

It would have to be taken out at midnight, well marked by a large star. I listened to her carefully and cautiously because this was another form of esotericism and its power, but I had nothing to lose.

To form the star, a compass would be required. The point of the figure had to be pointing to the north, and I would have to carry a yellow rag with me to mark the spot where the box of jewels would be placed at the moment of its retrieval. This was necessary to avoid anything going wrong because when the earth wall was broken, elves could appear and try to halt the proceedings. I had to put on a brave front and under no circumstances show fear. If the snake came out of the bottom of the well, I already knew how to break the spell. (The secret of fighting against a serpent under a spell is the following: with a dagger and a very sharp sword, you have to cut the head, which will spew forth coins—a very difficult thing to do but one that can only be achieved by the fearless.)

To obtain the exact location of the treasure, I had to use my rods and make a special ladder besides using the words of invocation that I already knew. Lucy also told me that I had to go to Mexico City and get the medallion of King Solomon's key and a black ring. After forming the star, I had to cover it with lime.

Her part of the deal was to transmute to be present. She told me that I would have to be careful because the owner of the land would be with me but lacked the courage to go down into the well. He would, however, help me do whatever I asked him. She advised me to take my pneumatic drill with me to be able to work more quickly because I would only have an hour to get the jewels out. I asked her who the client was, but she didn't want to tell me, adding that I didn't know him.

Everything would take place the following Tuesday, so it would be necessary for me to go to Mexico City straightaway to purchase the material. What surprised me more than anything else was when she said she would cover all the costs. She took out her purse and gave me more than enough to pay for everything. She explained that half of the bounty would be for the property owner, and the other half we would share between us. I agreed to that. She seemed very different when we were talking about that, almost as if she wasn't really there at all.

"If you want to take a bath, there's hot water, and we would be more comfortable," she said then.

"Let's leave that for another day. And when that moment comes, I'll make love to you like no one else has during your entire life."

"That's a promise that you're going to have to keep then," she said, smiling.

"I mean it," I said.

I thanked her for the food she'd cooked for me, and later in the afternoon, I went to see Nachita and told about everything I'd discussed with Lucy.

She told me to be careful about getting physically involved with Lucy, but with regard to the business proposition, she advised me to go ahead and see how it would work out. There was a buzz then in the crystal ball, and looking into it, she confirmed the presence of El Compadre.

"Dominik is here now and would like to know if you are going to let him take the treasure out of the well," she asked El Compadre.

The answer to that direct question was that the removal of the jewels was possible, but they couldn't be sold anywhere in Mexico; they would have to be sold in Europe. He assured her that this time he wouldn't oppose the removal of the treasure. I really didn't believe that, but I had to run the risk anyway. That same night I left for Mexico City to get the provisions required. There's a place near the Merced y de Granaditas market where articles of witchery that are banned everywhere else can be bought.

When I came back on Monday morning, I went to see Lucy, who was expecting me. It turned out that Montes was her client, a fact that she hadn't revealed to me for some reason. Their relationship was obviously discreet. I guessed they had their reasons, so I just went about my business of checking the site with my rods and made all the relevant adjustments.

When the day came to extract the jewelry, I discovered that Montes had drunk half a bottle of tequila to give him the guts to go ahead with the operation. It was a bad way to start proceedings and didn't augur well for the rest of the affair. Despite that, I was able to get the stone out of the well that was supposedly just above the box. But as there was nothing there, I used my rods and established that the jewelry had shifted farther down. Montes kept on pressuring me to dig deeper, but I said that in doing that, I would only force the box to slip farther down. Nevertheless, I continued, noting that the earth had that familiar burnt look about it, which indicated something was there. But as I suspected, it was all in vain as everything shifted farther below.

I wasn't surprised in the slightest that that had happened, and disgusted, I packed my tools up and put them back in the van. I saw Montes gesture to someone that I couldn't see, but I was in no mood to find out who else was there and slammed the door of my van and left never to return again.

I went to see Lucy at night, and she told me that she hadn't been able to transmute herself because El Compadre had stopped her from doing that. The incident had bothered her a lot because she was sure that she was going to be able to do that. I told her what happened with Montes; so she threw the snails again, and shaking her head, she said I was never going to see any more of him even though he would seek my help indirectly in the future.

My suspicions had been confirmed. I knew that Montes wouldn't play fair. Something had stopped us from going through with the operation. And trying to distract myself from that somber thought, I said, "If you want, I could stay with you tonight."

She said it would have to be another day because her daughter Betty was staying in the house. It would be a long time before I saw her again.

One day before the trip to Ciudad Victoria, Torres came around to confirm that we were going and came back the next day with his wife and children, who were only going as far as the house of their in-laws. We stayed with them there that first night.

We continued early the next morning, and Torres's brother-in-law, an easygoing chap, accompanied us. His presence in the car made the trip go much quicker than it normally would have as we spoke about a wide range of subjects.

When we arrived in Ciudad Victoria, it took us quite a long time to locate the house we were looking for. A large dwelling, it had two statues in the middle of the garden: one of San Judas Tadeo and the other the Virgin of Guadalupe.

We were received by Leticia, an attractive woman around fifty years old. She talked to Torres alone for around thirty minutes and then with his brother-in-law for another twenty minutes. I entered her rooms then and stayed with her for more than an hour because we not only talked about the treasure buried at Torres's ranch, but she also advised me about the folly of making pacts with El Compadre. She could see through her crystal ball that I was going to be very rich, but she couldn't discern the source of that wealth. She also saw that I had been carrying a very heavy cross for a period of thirteen years. That obviously referred to my matrimonial problems, and the number thirteen was right because I had lived overseas for five of my eighteen years of married life. She'd managed to hit the nail on the head!

She also saw that many people would be helping me to overcome the dangers that I would have to face soon. She couldn't tell me who those people were, and I could not imagine their identity. She foresaw the end of my marriage and said that after a year or two, I would meet the woman of my dreams unexpectedly, and this woman wouldn't be Mexican but from a country a long way away. How far, she couldn't tell me. This comment set her apart from Lucy, from Margarita, and even from Nachita. Her prediction surprised me, and I sensed only time would resolve the doubt I felt. (It should be pointed out here that after settling in the United States after this adventure was over, I met a Colombian through the Internet and traveled to her country. We were together for four years.)

This woman also divined that I had energy inside me that she couldn't understand. She assured me, however, that she would have another look during the night for the source of that energy and would explain her findings to me the next time we met. During the conversation, I observed how she used the pendulum to form questions that were then responded to. She told me that my rods were very good and that I must look after them well; and she also said that in the house at Las Aguacates, there was also a burial site, which she suggested we should start on first.

She was also aware of the great amount of money that had been spent to keep everything going and could see my anger in not being able to shake the bar of gold free. She told me not to feel too bad about that because if I had been able to take it out, somebody on the surface would have paid for that action with their lives. The serpent was there, acting as guardian to the bounty, and the situation could have deteriorated very quickly. She encouraged me to continue, however, and said that Torres and I were going to be very good friends and that despite his wealth Torres would have need of my support in the future.

In truth, I was very grateful to Torres for having taken me to see this woman. I thanked him as we got in the car to start the journey back. He asked me on the way, half jokingly, if Leticia had held my hand during my meeting with her. I told him more than just her hand, and he roared with laughter. I also told him that being with her had been so engrossing that I had lost all sense of time. We didn't talk about what was ahead of us, most probably because he didn't want his brother-in-law to know about that. Once we got back to Tamazunchale, he told me that seeing we were close to the New Year festivities, it would be better to leave everything until the middle of the following month. He handed me a wad of money to keep me going until then, and we said good-bye.

I will speak now about the extraordinary things that were to happen next.

8

Excavation at the House in Los Aguacates

Once the New Year's celebrations were over, Don Torres came around to the workshop one morning and said we could go to Los Aguacates as soon as I was ready. He said he had no objection to me bringing Joaquin along if that was what I wanted.

I hurried through my work that morning because I had to go and fetch my rods from a friend's house, and I picked Joaquin up on the way, explaining as I was driving what needed to be done at Torres's place.

It was a large house in the older style set on two blocks. Torres was on the upper block when we arrived, and he took us to the backyard when we got there, where two avocado trees stood at opposite ends of the yard.

"Get your rods to give us a reading on what's under these," he said, smiling.

Taking one in each hand, I gave them a good shake to liberate the energy in them. I raised the palms of my hands, forming a heart; and the rods turned immediately, marking a direction. I looked to where they were pointing and walked to a point in the opposite direction and shook them again, and they repeated the same angle and the same point as before. I walked there, and the rods opened completely about a meter from the trees.

The rancher found all that very amusing, and he said that the point that the rods had marked was the very spot that his tenants had seen chickens coming out of and on other occasions a woman dressed in white, walking in circles around the site. It was the reason that no one dared go anywhere near the place at night. I took a sample of the earth and put it in a bag to take to Nachita and to Don Benito for analysis.

Torres announced that we would return to the site but only if Margarita accompanied us and that neither of us told her where the spot that I'd marked was. In this way, we could establish her esoteric powers. I agreed to that and left. Later that day, Torres came looking for me and asked me to go back with him but not to bring Joaquin this time. He could come later when he was needed. I agreed to that, and he left. (Joaquin is a simple person, but he has a hard edge to his nature, and I understood Torres's position.)

We met Margarita in the house at Los Aguacates the next day and went straight to the backyard where Torres asked her to locate the burial site without using her pendulum. Margarita took a box the size of a domino case out of her satchel. The box contained two billiard-type balls but with strange symbols written on their surface. She walked to the center of the yard, said a few words, and then threw the balls in the air. When they fell, they rolled to the exact spot that I had marked with my rods.

Torres looked me in the face with an expression that told me not to say anything to Margarita and then walked over to her and asked her what she thought the site could possibly contain. She told him there was a pot of gold buried at a depth of six meters, which she said she wouldn't charge us a cent for in helping us extract it. Torres told her that he'd let her know. We all left after that, but sometime later, Torres rang me on my cell phone to remind me to follow up the soil analysis with Nachita and Don Benito. He said he was going to see a shaman in Tanquián.

The next day I went to see Don Benito, and while we were talking, I told him about the property without mentioning who the owner was. He took the earth sample into his room, and when he came out ten minutes later, he said that the treasure buried there was very large indeed and that the pot was a type known as a Valentina. But the site was protected by a spirit, and for the moment, Don Benito couldn't see what that spirit wanted in return for releasing the treasure.

When I left the house on my way to Tamazunchale, I bumped into Lupe, who asked me if I was going to do another excavation with Nachita as consultant, and I told her that I was. She asked me to be introduced to her because something had happened, and she needed to get in touch with her. I asked her what it was all about, but she told me that she couldn't tell me anything, at least for the moment. In the presence of the other person, I would be able to find out.

I called Torres to tell him about the conversation, and he told me in his own way not to worry myself about things of little importance. If it involved shamans or clairvoyants, then I had his undivided attention. I told him I'd pass on any information I got from Nachita and wouldn't bother him anymore with Lupe's concerns unless it blew up into something more important.

In the afternoon I picked Joaquin up on the way to Nachita's house. It was a two-hour drive, and it was good to have some company. When we arrived, she invited us to have dinner with her family; and later, when we were alone, she asked me if I had brought my rods to check anything out on her property. There was buried treasure there, but she wasn't going to do anything about it because she considered herself to be in the service of El Compadre and she wasn't going to put the life of one of her grandchildren at risk.

Later, when I went into the consulting room after Joaquin, I told her about everything that had happened at Los Aguacates, outlining what Margarita had done and the evident mistrust that the owner had. Nachita looked into her crystal ball and observed that besides gold there were also the remains of a person who had been buried there (which explained the apparitions), and to enable this soul to rest in peace, it would be necessary for the owner to look for a priest who could conduct a novena for the tranquility of the spirit. At a later date, she would give further instructions to Torres and his gang of men about what they would have to do and the cleaning process that would have to be undertaken to permit the excavation to start.

While she was explaining the procedure to me, she visualized two men in the crystal ball. The men, she said, would be the ones who would do the digging. As paradoxical as it may seem, she said that I couldn't participate in the excavation. I could only be there as an observer and check things out with my rods.

Right then, the crystal ball sounded as if it had crashed into another sheet of glass. She looked into it and saw the figure of Don Torres consulting another clairvoyant about the treasure. Nachita said the other man only wanted to swindle us out of our money and that I should warn my friend because I was the person he trusted the most and would listen to me.

The next day I went looking for him to tell him everything that she and Don Benito had told me. I explained the indications that I had received, and he told me that he had just hired two trustworthy men for the excavation (these were the two figures that Nachita had seen in her crystal ball). I went home then and waited the two weeks that it would take Torres to prepare for this great adventure.

I was anxious, but the waiting time eventually came to its end. They made the novena, and the excavation was initiated two days later. As the workers were digging, it was clear to see that the earth was very soft at a depth of two meters. This was strange because the soil type was basically hard.

That night in my own home, after the digging had finished for the day, I couldn't help but feel excited about the prospect of what we were likely to find. I couldn't wait for the next day to come quickly enough and to hear from Don Torres about what was happening there. He rang me late in the afternoon to invite me to come around with my rods. I only had to give them a quick shake when I arrived, and they gave a clear and immediate signal that we were close to the bounty.

They hit a slab of rock not long after that, which resisted all their attempts to dislodge it. So I lent a hand with my iron bar and tried to break it with all my strength. I gave it at least ten heavy blows, but the effort was in vain. It was immovable, and I felt exhausted and breathless, with a pain in my chest and a terrible headache. I was in a state of near collapse. They were all worried and helped me out of the cutting, and after a while, I came around.

My physical condition was excellent at that time. I could lift an eighty-kilo man up with one arm, and the bar only weighed twenty kilos. There was no good reason why I had caved in so badly down in the cutting, at least not looking for any answers with logical explanations.

As my concern persisted, I decided to visit Nachita the next day and tell her what had happened. My story prompted her to talk about the offering I needed to make to the spirit of the burial site. It was similar to most other offerings I had seen before: a tamal or patlache of seven meats (fish, sheep, pork, goat, horse, armadillo, and snake). Torres had to deliver the offering at midnight and make a hole in the wall of the cutting and speak to the spirit.

I went to see Torres after the visit to explain what was required; and in between listening to what I had to say, he told me about his meeting with the shaman, who also apparently had seen the need for an offering but at the point of confluence of the two rivers, where he would have to leave seven gold coins wrapped in a red cloth and a blank sheet of paper to receive the answer to his query.

That seemed unusual to me because spirits don't receive coins or money of any sort (even though they guard a lot). I told Torres what I thought, suggesting that a black mass or patlache was more in line with normal custom, and he agreed not to go ahead with what the shaman had suggested. Nevertheless, he went back to see him and ask who the spirit was and what it really wanted.

The second time the shaman told him to put a bottle with the blank sheet inside it at the confluence of the rivers. This didn't seem all that easy because where the *rios* Montezuma and Claro meet, there are large and very slippery rocks. Besides, to do that at midnight was downright dangerous. But being a rancher, Torres was used to taking risks, and he did it without complaining. It's worth mentioning that the current of the water there is dangerous even in daylight, so being able to do it at night was really extraordinary.

The following morning at ten, he went back to collect the bottle. He was anxious to know if there had been an answer. He ran back to the house without opening it. Whatever message there was could only be read in candlelight. When he finally took it out of the bottle, he was surprised to find that the writing was printed. Unable to contain his excitement and wanting to share the message with someone, he raced off to find me. I was in the town center at the time, buying supplies.

When he saw me, he said we needed to find Lupe straightaway; and when we found her, I introduced them. But before saying anything else, she proclaimed, "I am Captain Fontan. I belong to the army of Don Venustiano Carranza. My fellow soldiers and I collect gold from the crusades and then bury it with the objective of recovering it when the battle is over. We put the gold in a pot and bury it. Only the colonel and I know where it is buried, and it was in that very place that I was shot by the colonel and buried alongside the treasure. So that my soul can rest in peace and I can deliver this treasure to you, I need you to make me a patlache. Thanking you for your religious duties."

As soon as she'd exclaimed those words, she then described the person physically and then fainted. We took her to her house, and I carried her up the stairs to her room, which surprised Torres. "Ay, you're a strong lad. There's no doubt about that. I can't understand what happened to you at the cutting at my place."

Lupe had recovered her senses by the time Torres took the sheet of paper out of his pocket and read exactly what Lupe herself had just told us. That was simply amazing! It was a word-for-word copy of what she'd said. I left the house with Torres in silence, trying to come to terms with what had just happened.

A few days passed, and as the rancher hadn't come around to my place, I decided to visit him. I found him in a cantina, drinking. He seemed like a completely different person, and to top it off, the binge lasted two weeks. To say the least, I was worried about him, but I had no choice other than to wait for him to get sick of waking up every morning with a hangover.

I decided to go and see Nachita and tell her what was happening and to let her know how worried I was that the binge was lasting as long as it was. Besides, he'd seemed to have completely forgotten the commitment we'd made. Nachita told me to go and see him again and that this time he'd react when he saw me and remember what we'd agreed to do.

I went to the town the next day and found him drinking beer at the house of a friend. He seemed a little more sober than he had been and told me not to worry and that we would see each other the following day. I left wondering if that would happen or not.

He didn't show up the next day as he had promised but sent some workers instead in his damaged van, which he wanted put back in working order. Three days after I'd last seen him, he came looking for the vehicle and asked me how much he owed me, and I told him nothing. But he took an envelope out of his pocket and handed it to me. There was more money inside the envelope than my normal repair bill would have been. He told me not to worry about the money or anything else and that he'd advise me in advance when he was ready to go ahead with the ritual.

Watching my reaction to all that carefully, he said, "Listen, I love you more than one of my sons. Even my ex-wife doesn't get as much money as you do. You're never going to let me down, are you?"

I thanked him for what he'd just said because to be honest I could really only count my friends on one hand, and I promised him that whatever happened, we would always be friends. He seemed satisfied with that and left.

I waited several days until he called me to tell me that everything was ready and that we could carry out the ritual on Tuesday night. I informed Nachita of that, and to my surprise, she said that there could be no excavation work on the day of the ritual. Work could resume the following day, which was customary. I could be present but couldn't take part because if I did, my life would be at risk.

On that Tuesday at midnight, Don Torres conducted the ritual. He had to go alone because no one could accompany him, but as is his manner, he did that without much fuss. He is a very well-known and prosperous man of the region, which means that he has to exercise caution in everything he does, including arousing the suspicions of those living on his own property.

The work began again at the excavation site the following night. The rock slabs were that soft that the surface gave way as if they were made of clay or hardened mud. Everything seemed to be extraordinarily easy; but when the five-meter depth was reached, everything changed completely: the rocks at that depth were as good as unbreakable, and sparks flew from the shovels and picks, but the surface held firm. As a last resort, I advised them to take out the large mallet that we had brought along, but even that proved ineffective—nothing happened.

The only thing that faintly resembled progress was the hollow sound of the rock, which frustratingly permitted us to hear what sounded like coins rattling on the other side every time the mallet made contact with it.

My friend threw everything angrily on the ground and told me he was going to speak with Margarita and find out what he had to be done to meet El Compadre.

I went to see Nachita the following day. She told me she had observed everything through her crystal ball and explained that the way had closed again. El Compadre had made this last rock as hard as steel so that nothing could be taken out. She then gave me instructions about how Don Torres could speak with Lucifer. He would have to lock himself in a dark room with nothing but the light of a single white candle and invoke him at midnight; and most importantly, he had to summon new reserves of courage to empower himself to do that.

I relayed that information to Torres, and he told me that Margarita had said exactly the same. He was determined to do it even though he had no blood pact with the devil.

He took a few days to do all that, and I waited patiently. His workers came to my workshop one day and told me that when they were digging, they felt their backs being patted by a cold hand, which sent chills up their spines. Some of them said they couldn't continue anymore.

I went looking for Joaquin so that he would accompany me to the Devil's Cave after we had seen Nachita. I had another car that afternoon, a Nissan four-wheel drive.

I told Nachita that a lot of time had passed since I'd last spoken with Torres and that it seemed as if he was avoiding me. I only wanted to know if he had been able to speak with El Compadre, and she nodded that he had. But she told me not to put any pressure on him because he would tell me everything when he was ready to. I left it at that and told her that we were going to the Devil's Cave and that Joaquin knew how to get there.

As far as the excavation at the house in Los Aguacates was concerned, Don Torres eventually summoned up the courage to tell me what had happened the night of the invocation after many days of total and absolute silence. "Dominik, I don't know if what happened was real or it was a dream, but I heard a voice that night that asked me if I wanted the treasure. It told me that if I did, I had to give an unequivocal yes as an answer, and the voice said the treasure would then be released to me. Only one thing would be asked for in return: my son's life! That's why I haven't gone back there and haven't laid a finger on anything at the sight."

He also asked me to accompany him on a visit he was about to make to another shaman.

9

First Ascent to a Haunted Mountain

The rainy season had arrived, and it had become hotter, reaching thirty-eight degree Celsius in the shade. The heat was hardly bearable as we made plans to leave for the Devil's Cave.

I had already talked with Nachita about this visit, about what I intended to do, about the urgent need I had to speak to El Compadre. She had consulted her crystal ball and spoken with Lucifer and heard his mocking laugh about me not having the courage to visit him in the cave. But I'd made my decision to go, so Nachita limited herself to describing all the dangers that could be encountered there, about the wild animals that lurked within.

The following morning we got everything together in the van and headed off. We passed through a town located on the banks of the Rio Claro, and as we were leaving, the van became bogged in a small muddy pool. I turned the double traction on, but we still couldn't get out. On the contrary, the wheels seemed to be deeper in the mire. The townspeople came to help us, but despite all their efforts, there was no moving the van. It seemed as if something was working against us reaching our destination. The pool was only small and not all that deep. It didn't make any sense that we couldn't pry our way free. Eventually, we were able to pull it out; but by the time we did, it was three in the afternoon and already too late to think of continuing on to our destination. We chose to go home instead with the intention of making an early start the next morning.

We took a longer more dangerous route the next day to avoid getting bogged again in the same mudhole.

We were both unusually anxious as we followed the banks of the Rio Claro until we decided to stop at one point and leave the van on one side of the river and swim to the other side because it was the only way to get across.

We walked from where we had crossed to a nearby town and asked the people there how to get to the Devil's Cave. They looked at us suspiciously, but one of them told us that we would need special knowledge of the local terrain to be able to get there because many had tried before and never come back, or when they did, it had been many days later. He explained that the mountain is very treacherous and that many people have disappeared mysteriously in the surrounding jungle.

The locals noted that I wasn't from the region and asked me if I wasn't afraid of never seeing my family and friends again. It wasn't the first time I'd been asked a question like that, and I told them I wasn't because I always found my way back one way or another.

I said that, of course, to sound positive more than anything else. What lay before us seemed like a fascinating adventure but one that was fraught with danger. But either way, we decided to head off straightaway and not waste time. We climbed the rocky face of the mountainside, which was very hard going; and when we got to the top, we encountered scrub that we had to cut our way through with machetes. We did that until we were about a hundred meters from the cave when everything changed again, and unbelievably, we arrived back at the starting point. We repeated that scaling-and-cutting process at least five times.

Naturally, I had started getting desperate and told Joaquin to stay close behind me as I cut my way through the undergrowth again. Just then, with our backs to the cliff, we began to break our machetes on great reeds covered with thorns and thistles, which led us in a new direction. I had the feeling that there was someone else behind us, but we pressed on just the same. Suddenly, we were shocked to see that we had found ourselves in a valley that was so beautiful that it seemed to have been taken out of a book of jungle tales. The trees were gigantic, and the screams of monkeys could be heard, but what was even more surprising was the roar of a lion! It came from a point not that far from where we were at that moment. We followed the track ahead of us because it seemed like the only way out of the valley and the only way to find the entrance to the cave.

We were exhausted and as desperate as I can ever remember being. Joaquin started to cry like a frightened small child. I told him to get hold of himself and that everything was going to work out all right. We kept walking, and soon we arrived at a spot where we felt like two dwarves standing beneath an enormous cascade but one without water. It was completely dry! I decided to go back another way, trusting in my intuition and my sense of direction. We started up the mountain again when it became obvious that we weren't going to leave the valley floor by any other means. What we achieved by doing that was to finish up at our original starting point, which seemed like a half a day before. To add to the oddity of the whole experience, the townsfolk were waiting there for us.

We sat down under a lime tree and began picking the fruit off the tree and eating as many as we could because we were hot, sweaty, and exhausted.

While we ate, I thought about what had happened that day, about the series of strange things that had occurred, and about the extraordinary fact that we had finished up, no matter which direction we had taken, in the very same place.

I felt that something or someone had been observing us from the very moment we'd started the climb, but I'd said nothing to Joaquin out of fear of frightening him unduly.

We decided to freshen up then in the river while the townsfolk peppered us with questions about what had happened on the mountain. They'd seen us come out at the top of the cliff face above and figured we must have seen something. We explained to them that the harder we had tried to find a way to the cave entrance, the more lost we'd become. They told us the same fate had happened to most of the others who'd gone in search of the cave.

We said good-bye to them and made our way back to the vehicle, mentally going over the nightmare we had just gone through.

After we got back to the van, I decided that I needed to see Nachita as soon as I could and tell her what had happened and find out why we hadn't been able to find the cave.

The whole thing had been confusing; and the next day, on the way to visiting Nachita, we bumped into Torres on the road near the entrance to his ranch. We told him what had happened on the mountain and that we were on our way to find out why we had been unsuccessful the day before.

When we got to Nachita's house, she told me that El Compadre had been behind us, causing the path forward to deviate so that we couldn't get to the cave. She said it had been a test of my courage and that when we came down the other side of the mountain, the lion's roar had come from the devil himself. He had found Joaquin's emotional collapse particularly pleasing.

I asked her why we hadn't been allowed to reach our objective when I had shown no sign of fear, and looking into her crystal ball again, she said that it would be possible in the future with different people involved and by following a different route.

She gave Joaquin a cleansing because of what he'd been through, but he still hasn't recovered from the episode.

My phone interrupted proceedings then. Torres wanted to see me and said he would be at his ranch on the weekend. I finished the call and then the session with Nachita.

We went back to the same place in the mountains two days later but this time searched for a little more information than we'd had the first time around. We discovered that there was another way there, which crossed several different mountains; and after taking that route, we found ourselves back again at the same point we'd been at the first time. But we continued until it started to become even riskier, and we realized that we needed better climbing equipment than we had.

We went back and tried again along a different track that we found, but this kept us too far away from our objective; and in the end, we had to accept the fact that all our new efforts had been in vain. I told Joaquin it was time to go back and talk with Nachita.

She told us more or less what I would have expected to hear: El Compadre was putting obstacles in our way. She felt that this was perhaps for the better because she wasn't convinced that I was ready to face what was in the cave, if and when we did finally get there.

I had to agree with her. I told her then about my conversation with Torres and what our plans were for his ranch. She said that was a more modest and reasonable goal, but in the end, the decision to go ahead with the rituals was the rancher's.

10

Rituals at Torres's Ranch

It was six in the morning when Torres rang to say that he'd be waiting for me at the ranch at two that afternoon. I told him about Joaquin and said that I would pick him up on the way. He was waiting for us at the front gate with one of his workers when we got there. When we arrived at the yard, Torres offered us a glass of cold pineapple juice then showed us around the property because I was only familiar with the part where the rituals had taken place.

After doing that, he took us to a lagoon where he asked me to take my rods out. After I'd shaken them, they pointed directly at a hill. There was so much energy liberated that goose bumps were racing up and down my extremities. I walked a mile away in the other direction, and when I took the rods out again, they marked the center of a flat lot where there was evidence of a dwelling that had been there some time before. Afterward, we walked back to the yard, and the rods marked another spot. Torres invited us into a *bohío* to eat because he'd ordered his staff to kill some hens for the barbecue that would be our lunch. He asked me which of the three points I'd located that I liked the most, and I told him the lot in the open field looked promising. That was apparently what Margarita had also told him.

He added that this time he would involve her in the search, but before that got underway, he was going to travel to the United States to buy a better satellite metal detector. When he returned, we would start together; and after that, we would go to Ciudad Victoria. He said he wanted us to use white magic for this new project.

There was plenty to think about on the way home.

(Author's note: A *bohío* is a sort of hut made of palms and bamboo and is typical of the ancient Huastecos that populated the area.)

I went directly from there with Joaquin to Platón Sánchez, and we managed to arrive just in time for dinner. It had been a gluttonous day to say the least.

Nachita wanted to know what had stopped us getting there earlier.

We explained what we'd been doing, and then she said, "Now you know why Don Torres didn't continue with that search at Los Aguacates. After all that, he doesn't want to consult me anymore. He's using another medium. He takes without giving. Mark my words, he'll get what he wants out of you in the future. You'll see. You'll support him because of the friendship. But keep your eyes open. Learn and observe. That will be of value to you in the future. Do you know that one of his brothers died when he was a child?"

Nachita told me the story then of Torres's rich father. The wealth had come from what the father had discovered, and apparently, the price he paid for that was the life of one of his sons.

Then she warned me, "Don't go digging. Leave that to the other workers. If you get involved, you may well finish up being the offering yourself."

"Will I see El Compadre one day?"

"At the moment you least expect to" was all she said.

We thanked her for dinner and left.

A week after, Torres returned from his trip, and he invited me to the ranch. It was time to test the new equipment he had bought, and I was impressed because metal objects were registered on a computer screen. Satisfied, we traveled the next day to Ciudad Victoria without Joaquin. I was pleased about that because I wanted to have another opportunity to speak to the clairvoyant there. We went into her consulting room together, and talking business, she said she would charge 10 percent for her part in the operation. She warned us, though, that there were going to be hurdles to cross and that under no circumstances should we give up. When I asked her why she had never answered any one of my phone calls, she said that each time she had tried to, she'd had a terrible headache that stopped her from ringing me.

On the way back, Torres rang Margarita and told her to pay special attention to what her cards were telling her because this time a good part of what we discovered would be for her. However, she said she wanted nothing in return and that she would play her part only to display what she could do if she had to.

I told them both that I would only go to see the progress of the excavation from time to time because I didn't want my presence there to present any problems with El Compadre. Torres insisted, however, that I come every day to check that everything was in order. Joaquin wasn't going to come with me because it wasn't necessary; and besides, he was away, doing a course.

Margarita explained how the night ritual was to be conducted and that I would have to be present. We would form a triangle with three blue candles marking the angles, with the three of us inside that space before the invocation began. In fact, the ritual was completed that very night.

It was very powerful indeed.

The materials used for the ritual are described on page 94. (Much care should be shown when using them; any sign of fear could prove fatal.)

Recite the following invocation with hope and fervor:

Great Invocation of Spirits with Whom a Pact Is Desired

Emperor Lucifer, owner and lord of all rebel spirits, I beseech you to treat my appeal to your great minister Lucifuge Rofocale favorably. I wish to make a pact with him, and I beseech you, Prince Beelzebub, that you protect me in my business. Oh, Count Ashtoreth, make the great Lucifer appear to me this night in his human form, without any pestiferous odor, and that I be conceded via the pact that I will now present all the wealth and gifts that I need.

Oh, Great Lucifer, I beseech you to leave your abode wherever that may be to come forth and speak to me, or if not, I will oblige you by the force of the great and powerful Alpha and Omega and of the angels of Light, Adonai, Elohim, and Jehovah to obey me. Obey me promptly, or you will be forever tormented by the force of the powerful words of Solomon's clavicle, by those which serve to oblige rebel spirits to receive their pacts; so appear therefore immediately, or I will torment you repeatedly through the power of the magic words of the clavicle: Agion, Telegran, Vaycheo, Stimulaton, Ezpares, Tetragrámaton, Oyram, Irion, Emmanuel, Cabaot, Adonai, I worship you and invoke you.

Be assured that as soon as these magic words have been pronounced, the spirit will appear.

When we lit the altar candles at midnight, Margarita said to me, "Dominik, stop thinking about what you are going to do with the money."

As incredible as it may seem, that was exactly what I was thinking about, so I put a lid on those thoughts straightaway and endeavored to think about something else.

She also said that this required a human sacrifice and would consist of selling a soul to the devil. She then said she would offer hers, to which I thought, *What sort of rubbish are you talking about if you have already been sold to the Santa Maria?* I didn't say anything, however. I simply shared an expression of doubt with Torres.

Later, I went to see Don Benito to tell him what was going on. He said that regardless of who was helping us or not, we needed to prepare a patlache in order to speak with the spirit and to find out what it wanted, and especially to do that at midnight. I told him that Margarita had said that we would be able to do the excavation during the day, which was something I doubted, and Benito told me that I should exercise caution and not put all my trust in Margarita. He also recommended that I carry the bottle with the potion in it that he had prepared for me at all times in case there was any escape of gas and also to consult him at any time if I needed to clear any doubt up.

After that, I went to see the rancher again to go over the preparations; and he told me that he had his doubts about Margarita as well, but regardless of the costs involved, he was prepared to give it a go. I told him that I was going to meet a woman that I had been told about called Leticia from the town of Tanquián.

11

A New Shaman from the City of Tanquián

Development of the Power of the Pendulum

Out for a stroll one morning, I bumped into Hidalgo. I told him what had been happening in my life; and he mentioned that there was a very good clairvoyant in the city of Taman, that it would be worth my while to pay her a visit and that he would accompany me there.

When we got to the Maria's house, we noticed that a lot of people were seated on chairs outside, waiting their turn to go in and see her. She is young and beautiful, and when it was my turn to meet her, there was an immediate attraction between us. In fact, we were both nervous. Her husband seemed a pleasant-enough person, but I could see straightaway that she was the one who ran the house and paid the bills.

I only had one reason for going there that day, and that was to find out if she could arrange a meeting with El Compadre. I wanted to know if she could use the pendulum to do that, and she asked me if I was sure that that was what I wanted to do. I told her that I was, and she said then that I shouldn't make any commitment with evil because it was a very heavy load to bear. I don't know why she felt the need to tell me that because I could see for myself that the whole process, while necessary, was still going to be unpleasant. Either way, she proceeded to summon him then.

What happened then was really amazing. The water in the fish bowl started to swirl, the speed of the El Compadre's response taking the woman by surprise. She asked him if I could use the pendulum, and he told her that I could but wanted to know what the person with her was offering in exchange for this dialogue. I focused my concentration on delivering someone else to his service: a vile individual with no regard for anyone other than himself. But the message relayed back via Maria was something else altogether: he wanted confirmation of a pact between us, which I immediately refused to be part of but asked him instead what would happen to all those who had laughed at me my whole life. Time, I was told, was on my side and would make all my critics envious of my future success.

Those who have the power of using the pendulum attract all others to them. In being given permission to use it, I was, in effect, being given a key to a whole new world. Before the link with El Compadre was cut, I was told that I would always be given answers to personal questions and that other shamans would come to me for the special knowledge that I possessed. The power of the pendulum would bring them to me.

I thanked Maria for having made what happened possible and offered her money, which she refused. She said she would help me in anything I needed.

Hidalgo entered then and asked his own personal questions, and then we left. The only negative in the whole experience was who I would consult first in the future: Maria or Nachita?

In the days that came after that, I used the pendulum again to answer more of Hidalgo's questions and was able to verify the answers. It told me everything. If a person was sick and came to see me, I could indicate the part of the body affected and establish at the same time which internal organs needed treatment. The range of things that I could do with the pendulum was simply amazing. I devoted a week to becoming familiar with it. Then I went back to practicing with my rods.

After this period of intense learning, I reached an agreement with Hidalgo and Joaquin to help Torres in everything he had to do, including the excavation. The agreement excluded me from physical participation, which gave them plenty to do.

We started to encounter certain difficulties during the excavation, so much so that I told Torres that something was happening. I didn't bother to consult Nachita, however, because she had warned me of the difficulties we would face. Because of that reluctance on my part to visit her, Torres suggested that I accompany him on a visit to another clairvoyant in Ciudad Victoria.

That woman told us that we were going to strike water and that it would pour out of the walls of the cutting, but we would still be able to continue because the water came from the branches of a spring. Under much of the surrounding land, underground streams flowed, and she explained how we could drain the water out. That was imperative because we were close to the bounty.

We did everything as she had told us, but we struck hard rock again.

Margarita didn't explain why the rock was as hard as it was and left to consult with her spirits to get an explanation. She was putting money into the project too, so there was no lack of incentive to get to the root of the problem. Before she left, we agreed to go to her consulting room the next day, where she'd let us know what the problem was.

When we got there in the morning, we discovered that she had written on large sheets of papyrus everything that El Compadre had told her we had to do. The ritual had to be enacted at Torres's ranch, and the entire house on the property had to be within a six-pointed circle that used demonic symbols.

The materials to be used were the same as in the previous ritual.

The invocation would be conducted in the following way: A hide of virgin goat, sacrificed on a Friday, would be placed on the ground, and upon that, a triangle in the form of route T would be traced with the magnetic stone. (This route is known generally as the treasure route but can, in reality, be considered to be under the denomination of route of eternity, infinity, the unknown, space, time, the occult, mystery, etc.) It is traced upon drawings of the great cabalistic circle or upon pacts. Talismans are placed under the calendars that support the blessed altar candles with three crowns of verbena, basil, or elderflower harvested on the night of San Juan to be placed on the sides. One of the plants alone may be used or any of the three indistinctively. The sign *JHS* and the crosses that are placed at its feet protect the invoked being from all spirits. As well, if the one who makes the invocation is sufficiently brave, invading spirits may also be suppressed.

When everything is in place, a metal bowl with live coals is placed at the head of the triangle where perfumes of incense and laurel are emitted. When that is done, at the stroke of midnight, the invokers will stand in the middle of the triangle, holding the mystery rod in the right hand with its great appellation to the spirit and in the left the key or clavicle of Solomon. The petition to be made, along with the pact and farewell to the spirit, is to be written beforehand.

When everything is carried out to perfection, the appellation is recited.

There were to be three virgins between the ages of fifteen and eighteen in the house. Although I asked myself how we were going to get these girls to come there on the day, Torres assured me that as they were going to be paid to attend. Margarita would have no problem getting them to come. Only Torres, the three girls, and I would participate in the ritual, with Margarita outside reciting the words of offering to deliver the virgins. I didn't know at the time but was to find out later that they would be offered into the service of Lucifer. This didn't involve them dying, but it still bothered me because I was unaware of the complete plan because Margarita hadn't allowed me to see the words of the incantation that she was going to make.

The arrangements were made and the food prepared, and when the time came, Margarita remained outside because she preferred it that way. Sex was on the agenda because an orgy was required at the stroke of midnight while Margarita was reciting the incantation. Nobody had told me that having sex was part of the deal, and as it didn't seem right, my head started spinning. That was why I went outside into the fresh air; and while I was walking around, trying to get a grip on what was going on, I saw a flash of light coming from the other house outside. It was then that I realized that the spell had been broken because I'd left the circle.

Margarita wasn't aware of any of that because she was about fifty meters from the house with the altar candles alight, reciting her invocation. Later, she told me that my altar candle had gone out suddenly, and she had to light it again and had sensed that my thinking had calmed because I hadn't left the house with the intention of destroying the ritual but simply because I hadn't felt well. I went back to the house and finished my part in the orgy, which lasted for another hour before we all collapsed exhausted. We slept the rest of the night, and the following morning, we all went home.

The excavation started again, and this time, I only went to watch. Cutting through the rocks was hard going—nothing was easy. The farther down the digging went, the more problems there were. Margarita suggested that the three of us meet that night to pray beside the altar candles. We met at midnight and linked hands, and she began the invocation in a very loud voice, "Oh, powerful Lucifer, god and prince, Prince of Darkness. We are here standing before you to beseech you humbly that you listen to our voice and bless us with your presence. If you do not reveal yourself, we will make use of words that can hurt you, those of Yahweh or Jehovah. You know also that that name is powerful, the one that provokes ire in you. For us not to invoke the highest god, we need you to appear. You who are so well known as Beelzebub, Lucifer, Satan, etc. Come forth and show us your power and let us see if we will or will not obtain this wealth that we are seeking. Once more, Lucifer, we beseech you to appear before us and be our guide to avoid us mentioning the words of the Almighty God."

After the oration, the flame of the altar candles gave off a light that was three or four times brighter than before, but mine had flickered, which made Margarita conclude that there was something in my thoughts that was impeding the resolution of the invocation and constricting the true petition of her words. I told her that I was honoring my commitment to the proceedings, but what I felt in my heart was something else.

Because of this, she indicated that we stop the invocation and go the following day to her house to permit the cards to be read again.

We did that, and she told Torres that I was, in effect, a bad influence on the excavation. My feelings regarding the secrets of witchery inhibited her ability to express her ideals in the invocations openly. I told him that as a result of that I would withdraw from the project to enable them to continue but that I would still be available if needed. I left them alone after that to digest what had been said. My role in the search for gold on that ranch was over, at least for now.

12

Excavation on My Property: Don Catarino and His Great Power

I met Hidalgo some days later. He wanted me to accompany him to visit a shaman that he had heard about who was apparently very powerful. I told him that I would go but only after seeing Doña Leticia and consulting her about some doubts I had concerning the property that my workshop was situated on.

When we got there, I asked her if there was anything buried on my property, and she indicated that there was; so I asked her, if everything was done correctly, would I be able to retrieve the treasure buried there?

She answered that I could and that I was going to meet someone who was going to help me a lot. I thought that over in the waiting room as Hidalgo took his turn inside.

After we left, and on the way to visit the shaman, we decided to take a detour through a village where there was someone Hidalgo wanted to introduce me to. The villager's name was Don Catarino, and he had the gift of being able to see the past and future through a diamond. He also cured people from incurable diseases. He was the local shaman, a very humble and simple man. His hut was a two-hour walk from the village, and when we got there, we had to wait our turn because there were a lot of people there to consult or be treated by him.

The walls of his consulting room attracted my attention when we eventually entered it, covered as they were with crucifixes and saints and Grecian mythological figures as well as his own photograph. He professed that his cures were based on the power of Christ, but I doubted the veracity of that.

When I was alone with him, he grasped his diamond and lit a candle; and looking at me, he said that he sensed a lot of energy emanating from me and that regardless of my present convictions, there was something on a grand scale protecting me from danger. I knew, more or less, what he was talking about.

I told him that I had learned the use of the pendulum as well as the rods I used in the search for gold. I asked him then if he was prepared to help me excavate the treasure that was buried on my property regardless of the costs involved. This time around, I wanted to do everything my way and not follow the custom of offering patlaches and lighting candles. It was going to be different, and hopefully, the result would be too.

He said he would help me.

To prepare for this new adventure, we made some trips into the mountains and visited several other sites that could help us better understand what was ahead of us.

We met shamans who had heard about me, and they asked me to show them some places where treasure was buried.

It was surprising to discover that even in unimaginable places, they knew about me. One of these shamans told me that I had to do something of vital importance for Hidalgo before beginning anything on my property. He also suggested that I go back and see Don Cata. That was something I did a little later, and Catarino told me that there was something unexplained about the energy of my companion, so I asked Hidalgo directly if he had previously carried out spiritual work.

He said that his mother-in-law was the one who had done that and that he had learned it, as well as being able to read the cards, from her. Don Cata told him that if he wanted to develop his power, he would have to be initiated in a simple ceremony. He seemed disposed to do whatever was required. But there was a twist to that at the end when Cata said I would have to be the one who conducted the ritual.

One single thought flashed through my mind: *What in the hell am I doing now, becoming a shaman myself?*

Putting such thoughts to one side, and before beginning any type of work on my property, I had to do what they had asked me. I followed the instructions they had given me for the ritual.

On the following day at the usual hour of the night, I asked Hidalgo to do the following, "You've got to cut your hand with this dagger and then write your full name in blood on a sheet of paper and say that you will give your whole life to the service of Lucifer. Pass this candle over the paper with your blood, and if it evaporates like water without leaving any ashes, then you've been accepted."

But nobody could have predicted what, in fact, happened; I was even surprised. The writing completely disappeared: there was no trace, no ashes, and no paper!

Once that was done, he read the words of the invocation, and then we went to our respective homes.

In the morning, we started preparing the site for digging. I decided to look for the town mechanic because I wanted to use heavy equipment such as professional excavators for the job. The price, though, was very high despite the fact that I figured the work could be done in two or three hours. My property measures between twenty-two and twenty-five meters long by fifteen meters wide, and the excavation was to be carried out on a site of fifteen square meters. I was pleased with my decision to go in this direction because I wanted to do something out of the ordinary to ensure the excavation's success.

When I returned home for dinner, my daughter told me that the blender had exploded and broken into pieces and crashed against the wall.

I believed her, of course. She never lies. Like her mother, she has a clear mind. I knew when she told me that this had happened because of what I was doing, and I decided to visit Leticia so that she could summon El Compadre and demand that he leave my family alone.

In the afternoon, my daughter asked me for the van to go to the college with her friends. However, in the afternoon, I felt there was something wrong because she usually returns early. My wife and the rest of the family had already told me to go and look for her and find out what happened. I was about to do that when she showed up without the van. When she saw me, she ran up to me and threw her arms around me and asked me to forgive her. It was obvious that something had happened, but I didn't rush her. I told her to calm down and not to worry because the most important thing was that she seemed to be physically all right. But she didn't stop crying, and her mother came out and tried to calm her down.

One of her friends told me then what had happened. There had been a terrible accident on the hill near the college. The friend told me that she had lost control of the van when she had tried to brake. Instead of doing that, the vehicle had accelerated and left the road, crashing into a tree. The van was broken in two by the force of the impact. The two friends escaped with bruises and minor cuts but still needed to be treated at the nearest hospital. Fortunately, the people who lived in a house near the accident scene had a car and were able to drive them to the hospital straightaway. The tree that they crashed into collapsed as a result of the accident and fell onto a vehicle parked on the other side of the road.

I drove to the scene then, and the police informed me that as it was my vehicle that caused the accident, the costs would be my responsibility.

They waited until the owner of the other car arrived, and he apparently knew who I was because of the details I gave him even though we didn't know each other personally. He told the police that he wouldn't press charges because he trusted me to repair the damage given that I was well known in the district for the quality of my work.

Either way, I was fined because my daughter had fled the scene of the accident.

The following morning, I went to see Don Cata, but he wasn't at home, so I continued to Leticia's house. According to her, the devil would leave me alone after this accident. I found that hard to believe, but from then on, there were no further incidents involving my family.

Before I left, she stroked me tenderly on the face and then kissed me. Nothing was said. She was young and attractive. What followed was predictable. I felt as if my whole body had been set on fire through pleasure. Despite the intensity of the experience, there was no follow-up. It was just a marvelous one-off experience.

The excavation was initiated by the heavy machinery on the day agreed to. Despite the power and weight of the excavators, the work was slow and laborious. It took a lot to get to a depth of one meter. The tractor shuddered and gave off loud metallic noises and was pushed to such an extent that some of the hoses broke. We decided to stop so the operator could repair it for the following day, and I took the opportunity to take the pendulum out and see if the machinery would be able to go deeper. The answer I received was in the affirmative.

I went to see Cata and tell him what was going on. He took the diamond out and looking into it discovered that there was not only one or two spirits trying to stop the excavation advancing but a whole legion of spirits. It wasn't as easy as El Compadre had indicated, but the treasure was coming up one way or the other because we were using heavy machinery.

As I could see that things were difficult, I went to see Torres's workers and offered to pay them to dig in places where the machinery was ineffective. They would have to take out rocks and stones from confined spaces. They accepted the deal, and as the tractor had only progressed three meters after a week's digging, I paid the contractor out and said we'd finish the job ourselves.

While we were working, Don Cata showed up and was able to see with the diamond that the treasure was wedged in a corner. We weren't far away from that. I went down and checked it out with the rods and marked the same place. Cata indicated that the spirit wanted to talk with Hidalgo personally to enable the excavation to continue. We would have to invoke the spirit at the usual time.

We met at midnight and lit the candle, but on this occasion, Hidalgo had to be present on his own as a test of his courage. He did that but failed to remember what had happened the next day at the excavation site. The whole experience had exhausted him to such an extent that he fell asleep for an hour in the cutting. The excavation, however, continued that day without any hitches.

But the next day we started striking honeycomb-patterned rocks that were sealed by red clay. The architect friends of mine who had been involved in the excavation at Lupe's house came to inspect the phenomenon, and as they were leaving, they invited me around to their house. They said there was a lot to talk about as strange things had been happening, and I assured them I would be there as soon as the work had finished for the day.

As things turned out, I went the following day, and they told me that in Chapulhuacanito there were several places where gold was buried. I told them that for the moment, I wasn't interested in another site but would take a look when I'd finished what I was doing on my property.

Back on the site the next day, we started hitting a very large convoluted rock that was very difficult to remove.

People came to visit us at the site to watch our progress, and one of these visitors was Don Roque, a rancher and businessman of the town. He had seen a giant snake enter his house and finish up hiding itself in the backyard. I knew that the reptile was marking a buried treasure site but at the same time wondered why people, like this man and even one of my staff, were beginning to seek me out to confirm the presence of buried treasure on their properties. I told Don Roque that I would go and have a look.

When work finished that day, I went over to Roque's place, which is about a half an hour's drive from Tamazunchale. I soon confirmed that there were several sites on the property but explained to him that I would have to finish the job on my property first before I could do anything about his.

I sought Margarita out later to tell her what was going on. She seemed impressed to know that we had reached a depth of five meters.

I had to buy equipment to enable us to extract the heavy rocks that we were breaking, and when that was done, we struck solid earth again at midday.

Don Roque and the architects came around again and could see a circular lid from above that was presumably covering something. But the picks weren't cutting through any more as the earth was very compact, so I suspended the excavation so everyone could rest while I went to fetch Don Cata.

On seeing the site, he exclaimed, "You've done it. You're only half a meter from the pot."

After he left, Margarita came around to conduct another ritual to ensure that the treasure didn't shift from where it was. I checked with Don Cata later to see if that ritual was in order. He said that it was and that I could feel confident now that the treasure would be brought to the surface.

Margarita gave me a list of materials that were needed for the ritual that night. There were the usual things on the list, but some seemed unprocurable: skull bones, candles, incense, opal stone, and stardust. Stardust? What in the hell was that?

These ingredients were not something that could be located in one day. I went to see Don Torres and told him what was happening. He advised me to go ahead with the ritual and he'd cover any financial shortfall.

I made the six-hour trip to Mexico City with Hidalgo. We didn't go to the famous market of Sonora as we had done previously because some of the items we were seeking were prohibited, which meant we had to procure them in a black market. Somebody asked me who we were going to kill with what we'd bought, and I told him no one; we only needed it to complete a job we had.

It was difficult to locate everything we were after, but in the end, we managed to and took it back to Margarita. We agreed to have the ceremony in two days' time because she said the preparations would be complicated, and then she said it would be carried out in broad daylight. That surprised me a lot because the rituals had always been enacted in the dark. Still, regardless of the oddity of her plan, we trusted in her judgment.

Nevertheless, what, in fact, happened was that Margarita showed up at my property at midnight prior to the convened ritual time. She conducted the ceremony with the materials that we had bought and offered a person's life. Not exactly for the purpose of digging the treasure up but, as we were to find out later, to make sure we weren't successful in doing that ourselves. We had no idea why she would have done that, and when we saw her pass by the property the next day without stopping, the mystery deepened. Curious, to say the least, Hidalgo, Joaquin, and I followed her in my van; and when we caught up with her, she told us she had something urgent to do in San Martin and would return later. Her behavior unnerved me because we weren't that far off the agreed time for the ritual, but she told me not to worry about that.

Taking the strangeness of everything into account, I let her continue without saying anything else but then took a shortcut to San Martin. I drove fast and got there before her, but she never arrived in San Martin. I called her by phone to tell her we were waiting for her at the property, but she told me she was in San Martin. I told her that wasn't true because that was exactly where I was! That must have shocked her because she left wherever she was and drove as fast as she could back to her own house. I rang a couple of my staff and told them to ring me as soon as they saw her pass by my property. In the meantime, I headed back as quickly as I could. They informed me when I made it back that she was five minutes ahead of me, heading in the direction of her house.

I rang her again and asked her why she hadn't stopped and asked her to explain what was going on. She said she had become involved in other situations and wouldn't continue with mine for the present. Her attitude irritated me, and I demanded that she give me a better explanation. But that was as far as the conversation went.

I couldn't catch up with her in the car; but I drove to her house, saw her van parked outside, and noted that she had put a chain on the door to stop anyone from entering. But that didn't bother me because I was wild with fury, and I went through to her consulting room but couldn't get from there to her living quarters. Her house is located at the foot of a mountain, and although I couldn't get to her home proper, I could see her from the angle I was at and called out to her to come up and talk to me. But she ignored me, so I started shouting insults because I had the strong suspicion that she was playing dirty. I eventually decided to leave but with the conviction that I would get the truth out of her one way or the other in the future.

I went to see Don Cata and ask him to investigate the reason for her behavior. He consulted his diamond and discovered that she had been on my property the night before the proposed ritual and, in fact, had offered a life in exchange for us not being able to bring the treasure up.

The shaman said that we should go to my property, and when we arrived, we could see from above the cutting that the lid of the pot was still there. The architects and Don Roque arrived then, all of them very excited about us finally having some success after so many fruitless attempts to unearth treasure.

"The treasure's still there," Don Cata said. "Something's going to happen. I can feel it. What have you got of Margarita's?"

"A document with her name on it and signed by her."

"Perfect," he said. "I'll be back in an hour before you go down."

I grabbed a mace that was in the cutting and started to strike the stone cover. While I was doing that, we could all hear the rattling of coins on the other side. I wasn't worried now by what might happen to me. But a short while later, I started to feel light-headed and told my helpers to go on without me.

When Don Cata came back, he said, "Dominik, when you've unearthed what's there, regardless of whatever happens afterward, you've got to bury this note with her signature on it. I've already done what I had to do with it." Then he handed the note to me.

I kept the document in my back pocket, and we continued. It took us six hours to break the copper lid. Everybody had stepped back to let the air circulate. My compressor was working on batteries because I didn't want the gas to affect all of us there. We took the lid off very carefully and let it air. We even put a little alcohol on it and waited in the distance. Once we were sure that there was no gas, we took the lid off; and to our surprise, there were only ashes inside. No money—only burnt remains.

We all knew that there had been treasure there at some stage, but it was clear to see what remained now. Before I sealed it again, I rang Catarino because everybody had heard the sound of coins rattling before it was opened. The whole thing was weird.

Catarino cleared the doubt up. "Look, the treasure was moved because of the ritual that Margarita enacted and the life she offered. It's six meters farther down now."

"You know what, I'm not going on with this. We've already dug to a depth of six meters," I told him.

I took the piece of paper that involved Margarita out of my pocket and buried it. Everyone started shoveling dirt into the hole. To fill it in completely was going to take more than a day, but we managed to shovel two meters of earth into the cutting that miserable afternoon. I kept my spirits up as well as I could and just concentrated on the fact that this experience had been the closest we'd got so far to hitting pay dirt.

13

The Town of Chapulhuacanito

After this bitter experience, I decided to visit the architects in Chapulhuacanito. They introduced me to Dr. Holguin, a well-known doctor in the region. We drove around the town together, and I soon became aware of the fact that the people there knew who I was.

We started looking at several places that they suggested contained buried gold, and while they were showing me around, they told me a story about something that happened in the town during the great revolutionary battles. They showed me the remains of an old fort and its walls and quarters where soldiers had lived in those times. It is said that on the night of September 3, the Day of Santa Cruz, nobody left their homes because the sound of galloping horses and soldiers yelling could be heard outside as if a great fight were taking place, but nothing could be seen through the windows of the villagers' homes. There was no one there at all.

My curiosity had been aroused, and I took my rods out and walked to a house on the corner of the square. It looked like a good place to start, and I wasn't wrong. The rods marked something important there. I checked all the houses in the town at night so as not to arouse the suspicions of the townsfolk. I was told that in the portico of that first house on the corner, a very large cache of gold had been found, and the bricklayers who had been laying the foundations of the house didn't say anything to the owner because they were afraid of not getting a cut of the loot. So they sealed the spot with even more cement than normal, and as rumor has it, the gold is still in the same place today.

Later, we went up to a part of the hill where Dr. Holguin pointed to an immense tree that was in a large property across the street from his house. He told me that every year he saw a large flame burning there. The property was for sale, and intrigued, I pointed my rods in that direction. The magnetism that whatever was buried there produced was extraordinary. It didn't matter where I was standing: the rods registered the same huge attraction.

When we entered the doctor's house, he told me that they still heard strange noises from time to time; so I took my rods out again and checked the whole house over, and they registered something significant in his backyard.

"Are you going to take it out?" a neighbor of the doctor's asked him when we were upstairs on the wall.

The existence of the treasure somewhere in the house was apparently common knowledge.

"No, I don't think so," he answered. "He's only checking the place over to confirm what we already knew."

The rods had registered the site as important, but Dr. Holguin didn't believe in esotericism; so that when I marked the spot, he took a detector of his own out and confirmed it and then got a worker to start digging. The worker dug there for six months, but something seemed to happen to him because he fell ill and couldn't continue. He had already reached a depth of six meters before that happened. And later, when the doctor visited him at his home, the worker told him that he had heard a voice that threatened the life of his two sons if he continued digging, and frightened by the experience, he abandoned the site.

Holguin took what his employee had said seriously. He was not a man who was given to exaggeration, so the cutting was filled in. The people in this town were different to other townsfolk in that most of them had received a good education, and like Holguin's employee, they told the truth. That too influenced the doctor's decision.

During my stay in Chapulhuacanito, I also checked the architects' house out, and it registered something important under a pool of water. The signal produced by the rods was extremely strong, and the architects' mother told me that she'd seen a woman dressed in white walking around the site. She said that this apparition spoke to her on occasions and made gestures, but she had been too frightened to answer her.

As the architects knew Nachita, we visited her and told her what had been going on. She confirmed the burial site but saw our chances of success as minimal given that she sensed the architects to be afraid of the supernatural. That observation made other decisions easier in that I wasn't that keen on helping them because the work would entail the demolition of a substantial part of the house's foundations.

I also visited the house of one of the architects' friends where the rods registered the presence of something near a tree. One of the men there told me that he had a property where strange things were always happening. We went there and checked it out and found a likely site. I was very interested in this spot and returned with a shaman, who explained that the treasure was buried at a depth of one meter but that it could only be taken out by the owner of the property himself, who under no circumstances could show fear because the excavation could only proceed with the permission of the resident spirit.

This owner seemed willing to do all that, so I waited in my van while he prepared everything, expecting him to call me at any moment to help him with something. I was prepared to do that, but experience had shown me that something supernatural always occurred, and that happened with him. There was always something that stopped him from completing the excavation. He told me that there were times when his head was spinning, and he would fall to his knees in the dirt, unable to get up for a while and later was unable to lift the shovel up. And on other occasions, after pleading to be allowed to continue, torrential downpours put an end to everything.

Dr. Holguin sought me out again, wanting to know if I'd help him to dig the treasure up if he bought the property. I told him that there was no problem with that, but it would have to wait a while until I had finished what I was currently doing.

We passed impressive hillsides and precipices on the way to Chapulhuacanito. The doctor pointed out a spot, as we rounded a curve, where there was a cave where three men had buried sacks of gold coins many years before. However, mistrust and greed worked against them to such a degree that after sealing the treasure, they finished up killing each other. After that, others had tried to locate the bounty but had always given up because of the plethora of supernatural happenings that took place there.

Dr. Holguin doesn't believe in esotericism, but he told me that in the river below the slope that we were crossing, many years before, a man was leading mules loaded with sacks of gold across the river when both of the animals were carried away by the current. Much later, a humble family of the zone was strolling along the riverbank when they stumbled upon the sacks of gold. Overcome with joy at seeing all the gold and thinking that all their problems would disappear, in no time at all, they decided to take a part of the bounty with them and return later for the rest. But after agreeing among themselves to do that, a voice proclaimed, "Take it all or nothing!" Shocked by the experience of what appeared to be an invisible guardian giving them orders, they opted to leave the gold where they had found it; and on returning to their village, they told others what had happened. Driven by lust to find the bounty, a group of villagers returned but found nothing more than two hollow depressions in the ground where the sacks had once been.

Many people have searched the area with detectors in a vain search to locate the gold. But I knew that with my prowess with the rods that I would find it. But there was something about the whole thing that made me feel uncomfortable.

I eventually arrived at the cave that the doctor had told me about, and sure enough, at a point a meter or so from the entrance, the rods clearly marked a spot. But there had been a landslide that we had heard when we were approaching, and I could feel the presence of the supernatural. Holguin said that it didn't make any sense that there could have been a landslide in the area and one, in fact, that stopped us making our way into the cave. But regardless of whether it was possible or not, our way was blocked. We were carrying shovels and other excavation tools with us, but the rubble was way too much for two men to clear away.

It was a daunting experience because the trek down was incredibly exhausting although the landscape was indescribably beautiful. But there was no gaining entry into that cave on that day.

Holguin related other experiences he'd had on the way back. He knew about other sites where gold was buried, but after what had happened that day, I wasn't all that interested in listening to tales of more buried treasure waiting to be dug up. But he kept on telling his stories just the same, in particular, about a cave with two entrances where the treasure was buried in one of the walls. I was polite and didn't interrupt his story, but the next time I was going to make the effort of searching for sacks of gold, I wanted something more feasible than what I was listening to—an easy job, if that was possible.

I realized that I needed to know more about how to break the spells that were put on burial sites; the town, after all, was full of people who had profited well from having unearthed treasure. And what struck me as being particularly strange was the fact that supernatural events had occurred in the presence of the people I knew, even to those in my own excavation team, but never to me! I visited Nachita and Leticia and Catarino again and went deeper into the matter.

Dr. Holguin told me that he was going to demonstrate to me just how loaded with treasure the town was, and one day as we were out walking, my rods pointed straight at the window of a house.

"The owner of this house hasn't worked a day of his life," Holguin said. "And he's one of the wealthiest men in the town. And do you know why? Because he's got a compartment under his bed stuffed with gold bars!"

The man in question had lost his whole family from one night to the next, which indicated that he'd made a pact with El Compadre. It would seem that he swapped the family for the cache of gold that had made him rich. He was an embittered individual who bought what he wanted when he wanted it and supplemented the income from the interest on his fortune with money-lending activities.

We moved on from that house and bizarre story that went with it to a very large and beautiful hacienda. "The owner of this hacienda is a woman who found a pot of gold on top of the earth while she was walking alongside the road one day. She wrapped it in her shawl and disappeared for a time and then came back and bought all this area. She's also become the owner of a company that transports materials."

In fact, the area he was referring to is an immense ranch and the woman one of the wealthiest in the area. She was very lucky because she hadn't been looking for anything when she found the gold, but she knew how to get every cent of value out of her stroke of fortune.

Holguin assured me then that if he saw anything promising in a situation, he was going to give it all his attention. That was probably why he supported me through thick and thin even when some of the projects I undertook verged on the absurd or the near impossible.

After that conversation, I went to see Nachita again; and while I was sitting in the room outside, I saw a young well-built man leave her consulting room.

When I went in to see her, she told me to close the door behind me because she had something to show me. The man who'd just left had given her a gold bar as thanks for her part in helping him recover a treasure successfully.

She'd told these people that the treasure was under a *polin* (a square peg) in a corner of the property of the house. They had followed her instructions explicitly: carried out the ritual, made the patlache, and conducted the black mass she'd asked them to. She told me then that she would never sell the gold bar. I don't know if she eventually did. (What is certain is that some time later, she acquired large properties for cultivation for both herself and her children.)

She also told me about another person that she'd helped, who had sent his son to advise her that they couldn't successfully excavate the site they were working on even though she was able to perceive that they had. When someone doesn't fulfill a pact, they finish up worse off than they were. It wasn't too long after that incident that the person involved in the excavation paid the consequences.

I told her that I was going to try to make contact with El Compadre in some caves and other places that I'd been told about. The crystal ball started vibrating then, and the water started bubbling wildly. El Compadre wanted to make a pact with me.

I was told that I would be given the chance to talk with him and be granted permission to unearth a treasure. But all that was dependent upon me making a blood pact with him. My answer to that was in the negative. I was then offered the possibility of curing people through the art of prediction with the pendulum that I had been using. I told him, however, that I would only use the pendulum to communicate with him and to ascertain the meaning of some other things. The part of becoming a healer wasn't something I was seeking, but if I met anyone who needed help, I would send them straightaway to Nachita or Catarino or anyone else who had the power of curing.

That was accepted in part as he indicated that I would be able to ascertain if anyone was sick or not by using the pendulum along with isolating the organ or part of the body affected. I was also told that I should never refuse anyone who was seeking help. I accepted that without complaint.

I was also informed that Dr. Holguin would also be allowed to dig treasure up and that at a future date to be determined would be granted a session with El Compadre.

Around that time, I visited Don Cata, who asked me to get him some provisions he needed from Mexico City the next time I went there. I had planned to go the next day to purchase some items for my own workers and told him I would be happy to get him whatever he needed.

When I got home, I phoned Angelica to arrange a meeting with her when I got to Mexico City. She told me that she wanted to tell me about something that happened in her mother's house when I got there on the weekend.

Before I left, I went back to see Don Cata again. I knew that the man who was living with Angelica had used black magic to gain her favor, and I wanted Don Cata to use his own powers to reverse the spell on Angelica. He listened to my petition and a little while later told me that the man in question had left the house in the federal capital and that I should make the most of my opportunity when I got there because a lot of time was going to pass before I saw her again.

I arrived at Angelica's house early on Saturday morning. She was still half asleep and said she wasn't expecting me because she thought I would have gone to her mother's house first. She was only wearing a flimsy bathrobe that was nearly transparent but invited me in without worrying about putting anything else on. After a short while, she seemed a little embarrassed about the way I was looking at her, and she said she would have a bath because she still felt stiff after waking up. She said she felt stressed, and I told her to lie facedown and I would give her a massage. I asked her to get me some cream, and when she came back and lay down on the sofa, I lifted her bathrobe up. I ran a sponge over her and told her to relax then began rubbing the cream softly over all her body: between the toes, the legs, the thighs, the hips. I asked her to lift her head, and I took the robe off. She was still tense but was relaxing all the more as the minutes ticked by. She seemed to be unaware that I had taken my own clothes off. I straddled one leg over her and began to rub her back and removed her panties before I began to stroke her vagina. She was completely still now as I asked her to turn over. She asked me then when I had taken my own clothes off. I didn't answer her but started stroking her breasts and told her to close her eyes and concentrate on relaxing. I rubbed her whole body again, and she opened her legs when I told her to. I could sense her excitement just before I entered her and made love to her for the first time.

It was something that I had wanted to do for so long. She was so beautiful. And after the magic of that moment, we showered together and then went to her mother's house. That was the first and only time I ever touched her. No other opportunities ever presented themselves.

Her mother was tall with very white skin and had a wonderful singing voice as did her other daughter Betty who had one of the best voices I have ever heard. She would occasionally sing a cappella for me when I was there but nothing more than that.

Her mother told us then that during the last three days she had seen a woman dressed in white walking across the corridor at the bottom of the stairs when she had been making her way down. Although shocked, she'd kept her nerve because she sensed it might have been some sort of communication from her dead husband. She felt that she would be the next to go. I sat down with her and held her hand and told her to calm down. I said she was perfectly healthy but that I would speak with my esoteric friends about giving her something to make her feel stronger than she currently did. And Angy (which was the name her mother used when referring to her daughter) decided to add, "And Dominik is real good at giving massages."

Then the mother looked at me. "Very well, give me one, Dominik."

To tell the truth, I felt so hurt by Angelica's comment that I didn't know what to do. In the end, I gave her a discreet superficial massage.

I gave Angelica some money to go to the market and buy some food and discovered to my surprise when she came back that she was an excellent cook. The meal was exquisite, and when we were washing the plates up after eating, I think she regretted what she'd said earlier too.

It was a wonderful day, better than any other we'd spent together, and we finished up on the terrace singing ranch songs.

I left after that in good spirits and stayed the second day in Mexico City at my mother's house, bought what I'd come to buy, and returned the following day to Tamazunchale.

I visited Don Cata when I got back, and as I was about to hand over the articles I'd bought for him, and without even a word having been spoken, he said, "Well done, killer." He'd seen everything, in fine detail, through his magic diamond.

A few days later, I decided to visit Dr. Holguin in Chapulhuacanito and tell him about the goings-on. He listened to what I had to say and then told me about other burial sites that he'd been made aware of. But I told him I'd leave all that for the moment because I was going to have a look at a few sites that I'd been told about in the mountains.

14

Excavation in Remote Places Where Rituals Are Performed

The first site I checked out was a cave in Rio Claro. I had heard that El Compadre rode through the surrounding bush on a stallion. I went with Joaquin on that occasion, looking around the area, making the acquaintance of the local population. We met one family that was very helpful; and although it proved difficult to persuade the mister of the house to be our guide, he eventually relented and took us to the grotto we'd been looking for, which was, in fact, on his property.

The cave entrance was triangular as if a great upward-pointing crack had fractured the rock face. I went in alone and found candles, the remains of sacrificed animals, spilt blood, and satanic symbols on the walls. High up, on the roof of the cave, light entered through a small aperture. The grotto itself was not all that big, and looking around, I could see no evidence of anything to do with treasure there.

It was a site where satanic rituals were enacted and sacrifices offered. Even after a short while there, my head started spinning, and I felt queasy in the stomach. The whole place disturbed me so much that when I went out I told Joaquin to stay where he was.

I thanked our guide, and he suggested that I keep walking upriver and talk with the people in the next village because they knew about a similar site where supernatural events had taken place. I passed that information on to Joaquin but suggested that we do that another day because I wasn't feeling well, and the level of the river had gone up a little, and it was going to make our return more difficult. In fact, we got stuck halfway just the same, and it wasn't until some of the locals got in the van to give us some more weight that we were able to force our way across.

On the way down the slope from the Rio Claro, we bumped into Lupe by chance and offered her a lift home. On the way there, we passed one of my wife's relatives; and by the time I got back to my place, word had got back to my wife, and a great row ensued about me being in the van with Lupe. In a strange sort of way, I didn't really care because we were living almost separate lives, and most days there was one problem or another to contend with.

None of that, however, affected my searching for treasure; that went on unabated.

A few days later, I met Don Roque one afternoon, and he told me that he wanted to introduce me to a woman who had been asking about me. We made a date to visit her the following Saturday when I knew that my wife would be away.

In fact, it wasn't just that she would be away. She had finally broken up with me and was going to the United States and taking my daughter with her. I agreed to her going and not to fight over the division of assets. I wanted to wipe the slate clean and make a fresh start.

I can't describe my feelings well about this change in my life. We had lived apart for five years earlier in the marriage, and we'd left the city for the country twice in an attempt to give our relationship a better chance of survival. I suppose that this final formal separation should have happened before, but for one reason or another, it didn't. Now my daughter was a woman, and soon she would have her own path in life. I didn't feel depressed, but neither did I feel happy. I just felt that I had to devote myself to what had become the most important thing in my life now: the search for buried treasure.

The following weekend arrived, and I was keen to make a second attempt at meeting El Compadre in another cave. I went to Don Roque's to be presented to the woman that he had spoken about, and it turned out that she also possessed powers of clairvoyance. She had problems and was in a lot of pain; so I told her to come to my house, and we could talk everything over there.

She arrived later that afternoon. She was thirty-six years old and very pretty with a good figure. We had dinner together, and then I asked her to lie down. I started to use my pendulum and told her where the problem was that needed attending to. I started to touch her and could feel my hands burning as if they were on fire. As amazing as it seems, and at the same time completely unintentionally, I cured her then and there. It was something I'd promised myself I would never do, and I am still firmly against it today. I have used this power that I apparently have on other occasions but only when there had been no other option.

When she started to feel better, I gave her a massage, undressing her as I went. She asked me then if I was going to make love to her, and I replied that it seemed like a good idea.

It was an unforgettable night, and I drove her as close to her home as I could later, and I never saw her again.

The next day, when I left my home, I was surprised to see Torres's van parked in front of Lulu's house. But when I saw him, I didn't ask him what he was doing there. We just spoke about everything else we'd been doing.

I was very relaxed that day. Lulu came to the workshop later to ask me how everything was going in regard to the excavation at Torres's ranch. I told her that, in effect, nothing was happening because the subject hadn't been brought up for some time. While I was telling her that, it struck me as a good idea to not tell her anything at all even if there had been something to report. Lulu had plenty of rancher friends, and many of them weren't friendly with Torres.

She told me that she had noted that I had the ability to develop a gift, one that involved seeing and knowing things that weren't accessible to others. She advised me to buy some tarot cards. I took her advice and started working with a pack that I bought. At first, the effort gave me a bad headache, so I preferred to keep them hidden for a while.

Lulu told me that she needed my help to do a deal with a rancher. She sensed that I could help her do that. I really didn't believe a word of that, but I told her I would help her though not at the present. I had too much happening in my life to put something extra on my plate like that.

Don Catarino came to my workshop the next day to ask me if I considered myself a shaman now. He told me that his diamond had shown him the possibility that I was able to see more things than most. He had also seen certain events in my future, the most important of which was that shamans couldn't offer advice or be consulted on Sundays. Surprisingly, he had seen that that wouldn't be my case.

I told him a series of things then, all of which were true; but this sudden flood of insights into everything around me was a two-sided coin: I liked having a gift like that, but it scared me too because it carried me into a world that I had never wanted to enter.

The following Saturday Joaquin picked me up after I'd finished work, and we headed off to Rio Claro again. This time we went to a village that was even farther away.

We found out through talking with the people of this community that there was a small opening about a half a meter wide and a meter high at the summit of a nearby mountain. We were told that if we crawled in, we would get to a large vault where many things have happened, but in recent years no one had dared enter for fear that something bad would happen to them. They didn't make any reference to anything buried on the site but just to supernatural happenings.

After several hours of hiking, climbing, and the occasional stumble, we arrived there. At that time of the year, the land was very arid. In fact, we thought that we had arrived at the wrong place, but some shepherds who happened to be near the summit at the time told us we hadn't made a mistake.

I put my backpack in front of me and crawled in. I'd brought a lamp in case we had vision problems once we reached the vault inside. After a short crawl, I found myself in an immense open space that gave me the sensation of having entered another world. I crossed the floor without being aware that I was going downward. There were no hieroglyphics on the walls, but there were burnt-out candles and a star painted on the ground and what seemed to be the remains of a turkey. Dry blood and bones and feathers were scattered everywhere. The nausea that I'd had in the other cave came back again along with the spinning head. I went back out and told Joaquin that there was no point in continuing because there was nothing of any importance inside.

The villagers had told us that if we followed the slope to the right, we would arrive in another community where the presence of treasure was common knowledge. Also, there was a very dangerous cave site there that was reached by following a rocky path. Joaquin and I decided to leave it for another day because we were both tired and it was already very late. We'd been able to do everything we had because at that time of the year it got dark very late.

When we were on the way back in the van, we met the two shamans who had helped us in the excavation at Lupe's house, and we offered them a lift. On the way, they talked about the "Lord" (the name they give to El Compadre) and told us that he'd appeared to them and indicated where a large cache of gold was buried. One of them was a sort of witch, and I sensed that he was a particularly cold-blooded individual because part of the deal for unearthing a cache of treasure a few years before was offering a few members of his own family in exchange.

The new cache they'd located had a price of thirty-four heads on it, a figure that was even too audacious for the cold-blooded shaman. He'd tried to have the number reduced unsuccessfully with El Compadre.

This individual told me that he could show me the site but advised me that he wasn't prepared to sacrifice anyone else now. They left the car then and walked off the road and down a hill and disappeared from sight. I continued on my way and made a deal with Joaquin before we got home to make a new trip to the site we'd just been told about.

A week later, we did just that. We found the rocky track, and as we made our way along it, I felt as if someone was watching us. We could see the cave from the point of the hillside that we were on, about two kilometers away. We then made repeated attempts to get to the cave entrance but weren't even able to get close.

We passed a man on the way who told us how difficult it was to make it to the cave. He suggested we'd have more success if we changed tracks. He also told us about a boy who had, in fact, entered the cave and on seeing the wealth within decided to return to his home to collect some sacks that would help him carry the gold better. But when he made his way back, he couldn't find the cave entrance a second time and eventually gave up after days of searching in vain. We could see the site clearly from where we were standing, but getting there was something else.

I went to see Nachita again, and she confirmed that the cave was under a spell and that for the moment access had been denied me. After talking with her for a while, Joaquin and I decided to concentrate on other sites that we'd heard about.

Many people had spoken about a gallery at the edge of a riverbank that was accessible only when the river current was low. It sounded like a dangerous place, and, in fact, many had been trapped inside by the rising waters.

I went to see Lulu to get her to use her power and energy to see if she could see what was happening inside this river gallery. She explained that a subterranean river flowed within the cavern and that the people who had lost their lives there were victims of natural phenomena, not through mysticism. There was little point risking our lives by entering that cave.

Later, she told me that she could foresee problems with my family, which I found hard to believe seeing that they had already gone to the United States.

At some point in the next few days, a schoolteacher called Conchita phoned me. She said she was keen to see me because she was going through a bad period in her marriage as well. Conchita has three children and lives close to my mother's house. I told her I'd make a special trip to Mexico City to visit her without letting anyone else, especially my mother, know. I drove there early one morning and brought her back to Tamazunchale and showed her around a part of Mexico that she was unfamiliar with.

She was great company, and we had a wonderful day. She is a very attractive woman, with a good figure, an instructor in volleyball and gymnastics. She stayed with me that night, and we made love even though we both knew that thoughts of anything permanent were out of the question. I was still in the process of getting my divorce, and she was still living in the same house as her husband but sleeping in separate rooms.

After taking her home, I was surprised to find out that my wife had returned from the States because she'd had big problems with my daughter, who wanted to get married. They were both at home when I got back from Mexico City, and even though I had a photo of Conchita on the bench, my wife didn't seem to know who she was. I thought that was strange.

In the days that followed, my wife tried to get me out of the house with her family's help, but I stood my ground. I'd already had my share of problems with them, and I had no intention of leaving that easily. I had to give her money so that she could go back to the United States and I could concentrate on my treasure hunting.

I needed to see Nachita after everything that had happened. I was thinking more about completing a successful excavation all the time, and I needed her help to do that. I wasn't worried about costs—I wanted results!

Hidalgo had called around to tell me that extraordinary things were happening on the property of Don Santos in the town on the other side of San Martin. The people there had apparently heard of me because I was the only person at that time who was exploring and undertaking excavations. I told him that before I did anything, I was going to consult Nachita.

Although there was thunder and lightning all the way, it only rained a little driving to Nachita's house. I had taken the jeep, and I always had the vehicle in optimum mechanical condition when I went on excursions through the mountains. Nevertheless, it stopped along the way as if the battery had suddenly gone flat. It was getting late when that happened, so I consulted the pendulum to see if we would get to Nachita's that afternoon. It indicated that we wouldn't make it, so I asked if we should take the way back. On seeing that the answer was in the affirmative, I put the key back in the ignition and started the jeep again as if nothing had been wrong in the first place. The next day I checked all the wires in great detail to understand what could have happened the previous day, but I couldn't find anything wrong with the battery. Joaquin and Hidalgo were amazed by the whole affair.

After that, and all the other adventures that Joaquin and I had been in together, he told me that he didn't want to continue anymore. He had problems at home, he needed money, and he'd been offered a good job in San Luis Potosi. I couldn't help him with the amount of money he needed, so I just accepted his decision as being in his best interests. From then on, Hidalgo became my right-hand man. He accompanied me everywhere as well as worked with me. Two of Don Torres's workers also helped out a lot although one of them dropped out fairly quickly.

We visited Don Catarino to ask him his opinion about why we hadn't been able to see Nachita that night, and he explained that it was simply because of the climatic conditions. Later that night, a landslide on the road caused a terrible accident. That sort of thing is fairly typical in our area, and the roads are so precipitous that if we had continued earlier and I had not consulted the pendulum, we would have more than likely finished up at the bottom of a gorge somewhere!

Don Catarino could see that we were getting closer all the time to El Compadre, and he asked us to do him a favor when we finally made contact. He said he was prepared to do whatever was required to avoid accidents happening along the surrounding mountain roads, and he wanted us to pass that sentiment on whenever we could.

I didn't have any problem with passing his message on but was confused by the nature of his request. Who did Catarino plan to offer El Compadre in return for the granting of his request? Was he going to offer himself or one of his enemies?

I took the road back to Nachita's house again, but on the way, I met Dr. Holguin on the side of the road beside his car, which had broken down. I stopped to help him. He said he was looking for us when his car broke down. The whole thing, on top of what had happened to me the previous day, seemed mysterious to say the least. While I was trying to get his vehicle roadworthy again, he told me about another village beyond Chapulhuacanito where the local shamans were interested in making contact with me. It seemed my fame had traveled as far as that remote place.

We started off for that place the same day, and asking for directions to the homes of the shamans we were going to visit, we met a woman with a very strange expression on her face. She told us that she knew what we were looking for because she devoted herself to seeing things and to carrying out spiritual work. We went to her house where she told us that she was very sick and had been fasting for three days before meeting El Compadre. That interested me, but she said that if we wanted to meet him, we would have to do likewise. I said I was willing to do that, but I needed her guidance so the right steps could be followed. However, she said for the moment it would have to wait because of the delicate nature of her own health. She said that I should consult other shamans although she doubted they would be brave enough to go through with it.

I sought those shamans out just the same but realized that they wanted us to help them dig up treasure that was buried behind their house. Every time they had tried on their own, the bounty had shifted. I told them I'd mention it to El Compadre the next time I had the opportunity to, but for the time being, there was nothing I could do. To be honest, I wasn't that interested in their project and didn't want to waste any more of my time.

Hidalgo and I left, but after all the events of the day, it was late, and we put the visit to Nachita's place on hold for another day.

When I did get to see her, she told me again that she could see that I had big problems at home. In effect, one of my sisters-in-law had been bothered by the breakup of the marriage. I was always closer to her than to any of my other in-laws. But she had changed after the separation and wanted to humiliate me as much as she could. I just took it in my own way and said nothing back to her when she launched her tirades against me. But I went to see Don Cata; and although I was against the idea of using magic to harm anyone, on this occasion, I wanted Catarino to get my sister-in-law to leave me alone.

What I asked the shaman to do was to have a look and see if my sister-in-law's husband had had any sexual relationships with other women during his marriage. The answer to that question was that he had, so I wanted that to come out and see if my sister-in-law was capable of preaching against her own husband the same way that she had been doing to me. Don Cata said the whole family was in for a big shock in the next few days.

There was also another situation with my other brother-in-law and his wife who had been a prostitute when they had first met. She'd caused me plenty of problems, and I knew that she had been sleeping around. Don Cata discovered that she'd had a relationship with a man who worked for a catering company in the city, and I made the mistake of telling my brother-in-law just that. He said that his wife was hot-blooded, and he couldn't be sitting around all day guarding her. But he said that he'd be happy to sue me for slander if I didn't have any proof about what I was alleging. I told him I'd give him the proof in due course.

In fact, that's exactly what I did, thanks to Don Cata. All the family hypocrisy came to light, and in the process, I managed to kill two birds with one stone. This is what happened: my other sister-in-law found out about her husband's two-timing the same week. I wrote a question on a piece of paper that I put to the pendulum about telling my ex-wife the truth or not about what was going on when she returned from the United States. It indicated to me that I shouldn't tell anyone, but when she did come back, she went through all my things in the house and found the piece of paper with my consultation on it. You can imagine her reaction on seeing that because her return from the United States had been motivated by the fracas that was going on in her sister's house.

Her sister's health had been compromised by the scandal, and after reading what I had written on the piece of paper, my ex-wife asked me if I had had anything to do with whole sordid affair. I told her that I'd had nothing to do with it although I knew that the husband had been cheating on his wife, that I had never said anything because the rest of the family thought he was a saint.

My sister-in-law actually came to see me and asked me what she should do. I told her to face up to things as they were and forgive her husband because he maintained the house and their three children. I suggested that she try to rebuild the relationship. She took my advice, but what I really wanted to do was to pay her back for what she'd said about me. I wanted her to see her own hypocrisy for what it really was.

The whole thing finished with that, and they didn't bother me again. On the contrary, from then on, they were all a little scared of me.

Sometime later I went to visit Nachita again, and she told me about a new direction that was going to appear for me shortly and that it would be Don Cata who would help me to take it.

When I got home that day, I told Hidalgo to get everything ready for a trip to Mexico City. There were a few things there that I wanted that had been recommended to me by Don Cata, but I'd completely forgotten about them until that very moment. Why I hadn't remembered them before, I don't know. I also wanted to scout around there for a pyramid with a resin base. It had to have some gold in it and other elements that I couldn't quite specify right then.

On that occasion, I didn't tell anyone about us going. I didn't like the idea of my family knowing about my whereabouts at any given moment of the day; so we stayed in a hotel, and I was able to find the object I was looking for the next day. I was going to give it to Torres. It would be kept at his bedside when he slept.

On the way back, my van broke down in the mountains. We came to a stop on a curve where there was a little house made of sold materials, and the owners put us up for the night and helped us get alternative transport home the next day. The van stayed where it was.

I'd checked the vehicle over that morning and realized that the weather chain had broken. I knew I could get the tools I needed to fix the problem in Tamazunchale, but we needed to get moving because it was a two-and-a-half-hour drive by road. We got a lift home, bought what was required, and came back in another car and repaired the van.

The lady of the house noted my rods while we were talking and asked me if I used them to search for gold. After I confirmed that, she told me about some strange dreams she'd been having about a plot of land located in front of the house. I checked the spot out with the rods and discovered that aside from being strange, her dreams were prophetic as well. There was no doubt that something big was buried there.

I told her that she had to keep its presence under wraps and only tell one of her children or someone of absolute confidence to buy the equipment she would need to start any future excavation. I didn't offer her my help directly because I'd been involved in so many excavations up to that point that I felt like I needed a break. Besides, I was in a sort of crisis of religious conscience at that moment.

The woman's children made a note of my details, and three days later, they arrived at my home so I could take them to see Nachita. They had brought earth samples with them, and my adviser told them if they followed her instructions faithfully, they would be able to retrieve the treasure. But the request to dig the treasure up had to come from the lady of the house, and when she did that, she would have to show a rare brand of courage. Her children could do the digging, but she was the one who would have to remove the lid of the pot. They seemed very happy with the advice offered and paid me handsomely for having set them on the path to success.

Later, Nachita told me that they visited her again and that while everything had gone well at first, things started to fall apart, and the affair didn't have its expected successful ending. They followed her instructions, but when they had nearly reached their objective, the weather changed and bolts of lightning flashed across the dark sky and the sound of carts rumbling into the cutting could be heard. The children didn't want to continue, but their mother did. She was the one who had the will, courage, and strength to go through with it; but her children wouldn't let her do that. They waited for the storm to abate, then filled the cutting in, and left.

Nachita assured me that they were on the verge of bringing the treasure up. A little bit more effort, and they would have been successful. Nobody was in danger because they had followed her instructions faithfully, but the children had lost their nerve.

To my surprise, two days later, after finding out what had happened, the family came and visited me at home. They brought cheese and regional sausages and were in a very friendly mood. They confirmed what Nachita had told me as being true and said that they'd decided not to proceed with the excavation. They invited me to visit them anytime that I was passing by, but that never happened. I never saw them again.

During the whole week, a lot of people visited me, wanting me to check their properties over with my rods. All these people seemed very well informed about my activities. They all knew that I could identify locations with consummate ease and also knew that until that moment I had never successfully dug anything of value up! Still, I was becoming very well paid for my spotting work, and that kept me motivated and determined to keep at it until I entered the winner's circle.

Around that time, an individual who had a dubious reputation visited me. There were plenty of stories going around about him being a dangerous customer. That was something I wasn't too sure about, but I listened to the advice of others who had told me to treat him carefully. He'd come to see me because he wanted me to pass my rods over his property and see what I could find.

When I went to his property, he offered me half of whatever he and I together could dig up. I was happy enough to check his property over, but I gave him the name of someone else to help him with any future excavations.

Then I asked him, if the moment of truth came and the "owner" of the treasure appeared and asked him to trade his wife or son in return for the treasure, would he be willing to do it? Not surprisingly, given what I'd already heard about him, he said that he would.

I suggested then that perhaps his family wasn't the thing that he loved the most and told him that El Compadre would know soon enough what it was that he really loved. And if he wanted the treasure, it would be that that he would have to give up in exchange!

That made him think, and he didn't say anything for a while, digesting what I had told him. I told him then that when he was ready, I would send someone along to help him. I already knew that he wouldn't be able to unearth his or any other treasure. But nevertheless, he didn't seem to mind me having been so direct with him and offered me his help if for any reason I needed it.

For some strange reason that I couldn't understand, after leaving his property, I remembered something that happened to me one day in another cave along the Rio Claro. While Hidalgo and I were going up a hillside, we saw two apes at the entrance to a cave at the very moment that a ritual was taking place. They got such a shock on seeing us there that the spell they were in the process of casting was broken, and the two apes were suddenly transformed into two Indians. In fact, they were two Nahua Indian shamans who retook the form of monkeys as they ran off.

It was an astonishing scene that caused me to have a splitting headache for several days after the incident. I had no interest in entering that cave right then; but we did return later and found the same thing that we had in the other caves: the remains of animals, stars painted on the cave floor, and candles. We didn't bother to stay very long inside.

15

Excavation in San Martin (The Last)

The last excavation that I carried out was in the town of San Martin, on the property of Don Simon.

Hidalgo told me that one of his friends wanted to see me and that Don Cata needed to talk to me as well. I went to see Catarino first; and by chance, the other person who wanted to see me, a certain Don Simon, was also there. We were all a bit surprised by the coincidence.

He told us about his two daughters, one nineteen years old and the other twenty-one. They both, it seemed, had been bothered by a spirit that called them and invited them to leave their house so they could be given something. Don Cata had cured them of many things and helped them with others, but he couldn't do anything about the treasure that apparently was buried on Simon's property because he had no spiritual permission to do anything there. He wanted me to do that instead.

141

I told him that I would be more than happy to go to the house. It wasn't an easy trip given the distance and time factor, which would take me away from my business for several days. Nevertheless, I jotted his details down and told him I'd go there as soon as I could. Simon was a simple, hardworking man. He made his living from the sale of the cheese and milk that his property produced.

It took me a while to get around to fulfilling my promise to the dairy farmer; but Hidalgo and I got to work, getting everything in order at the workshop, and we headed off to Simon's property within the week. We took Don Torres along for the ride, and one of his workers came with us to help out if required. I wasn't going to play an active part in any excavation carried out there, but I would be in the background, giving orders.

Before we set off, I asked Nachita what special arrangements were needed, if any; and without surprising me that much, she said the owner of the house would have to make a blood pact with El Compadre. When we got there, I told him that, and he offered no objections to the suggestion.

We got everything ready to start the excavation, and Simon agreed to write his name on a white sheet of paper in blood. But no matter how hard he tried, no blood flowed. After what seemed like a thousand attempts, all he managed to produce was one single drop. He had scratches and deep cuts all over his body, but no blood had appeared. It seemed impossible that something like that could happen, and none of us there had any idea what was happening. I figured, however, that the owner of the treasure was behind the mystery; he wasn't prepared to accept any pact made with Simon.

I began lugging my equipment to the house. It appeared that I was going to have to play a bigger role in the proceedings after all.

We started to work, but something very strange happened when they started digging. I fell into a deep coma-like sleep. They dug furiously while I slept like a log beside them. When they stopped, I woke up and checked their progress over.

Things were going well apart from my mysterious bout of sleepiness. Simon was a kind host and offered us something to eat at the side of the cutting, which, added to what we had brought ourselves, meant that lunch was a veritable banquet.

During two days of hard work, Simon's daughter fell ill. Hidalgo had to go and see his mother-in-law, who was a clairvoyant, and ask her why the girl was as sick as she so often was. According to Hidalgo's relative, the reason was that the resident spirit wanted her present at all times, which meant that the girl had been overexposed to the occult and needed spiritual cleansing. Hidalgo was able to do that. It was something that I couldn't do myself because I hadn't been instructed in the art in the first place, and I had no interest in learning it either.

Later on, however, things changed somewhat; and I learned the art of cleansing, including the memorization of all the words necessary for the performing of the ritual. I finished up doing it in my own way without using the herbs that characterized the process of healing of most of the shamans.

For several nights, the spirit forced the girl out of her bed, and I later found out that what it really wanted was for her to be present in the excavation. And the difficulties continued with that too. Sometimes the treasure was shifted to the side, and on others, it went farther down. It was really very difficult to not give the whole thing away. But Don Simon was tenacious in his resolve to keep on digging.

As the days passed, Simon's daughter became very sick indeed, and we started fearing for her life. I didn't want her to go down and ask for the treasure herself, but somehow she found the strength and the guts to do that. The spirit had wanted her involved in the excavation all along and told her that the treasure could be retrieved if she was there. By now, Simon had lost any doubts he had about the power of mysticism, and he told us that the decision was one his daughter would have to make. I advised him to think that over for a few days.

Several of Simon's neighbors began coming to the site regularly because they knew what we were looking for. Their presence there bothered Simon to such an extent that he said he was going to stop the excavation for a while and let everything cool down. I didn't want to interfere in his decisions, but I knew if he did that, any hope of retrieving the treasure would be lost.

Something similar happened with another family we knew in Rio Claro. A voice advised the lady of the house that treasure was buried under a section of the floor. We told them that we would be happy to help them but that the woman herself would have to do the digging. That scared her, but in this case, her daughter was prepared to substitute for her. But that wasn't possible as the job belonged to the mother. The woman begged us to do it ourselves and suggested that all that was involved was lifting up the floorboards and discovering the first pot. I warned her that if the treasure shifted, it wouldn't be our fault but hers because she hadn't found the courage to do it herself. So we proceeded under those conditions; and to our surprise, we found it without having hardly turned a rock over. But at the moment when we did that, the sound of stones crashing into one another could be heard, and then we saw the pot heading downward. The experience was shattering for the woman because all the wealth she was counting on simply disappeared before her very eyes.

That sad ending had been brought about by cowardice and panic. Another seven years would have to pass before a similar opportunity presented itself. And the same thing happened to Don Simon because although the excavation was close to its target, it shifted inexplicably, and they gave the hunt up. I left all my equipment there just the same because certain things were changing in my life, and I was starting to feel stronger and braver and more capable of doing it all myself.

16

First Expedition on Dr. Holguin's Mountain

Hidalgo and I decided to visit Dr. Holguin. He had told us about a beautiful mountain that was an hour's drive away from where he lived. Apparently, by following the river down to the right, we would come upon a cave that was famed for the supposed treasure that was buried there. Only trouble was that anyone who had ever entered the cave in search of the treasure had never come out again.

It was strange following his directions downriver because I felt as though I'd been there before, in my dreams to be precise. I recognized things along the way: odd rocks here and there and great trees hanging over the river. It was very hard going, and after many hours hiking, we still hadn't found the cave. People we passed along the way told us we were close, but for some inexplicable reason, we couldn't locate it.

When we eventually decided to give it away for another day, we stumbled upon it. We tried to enter, but as we did, we heard the sound of rocks falling inside. We were lucky to get out when we did. There was nothing unusual about what had just happened. It seemed to happen to me all the time. So much effort, so much sacrifice, only to come up empty-handed in the end. I told myself then and there that we had to do something to turn our fortune around; we had to find the secret of how to extract buried treasure!

We swapped that cave for others we'd heard about at Taman. They had the same infamous reputation as the one we'd just escaped from. Plenty went in; only a few came out. We stayed there a few days, sleeping in the van when we were tired. I wasn't in any mood to give up easily this time and wasn't going to head home until we'd found and entered the caves we'd been told about.

We met a local peasant whom we paid to help us in our search. But it wasn't easy even with his help. The way to the caves was guarded by the local villagers, more for public protection than anything else. They didn't want anyone else dying there.

The site was at the confluence of two rivers in the middle of the mountains; and for many years, legend had it that a giant pot of treasure stood at the entrance to the cave, but it was always guarded by an enormous serpent.

The mouth of the cave could be clearly seen from higher up the mountain as could the giant pot. We got there on a night without moonlight, but although it was very dark, something was shining in the center of what appeared to be black and gold rings twisted around the pot. We were still a fair distance away, and the light from the powerful torch I had was able to illuminate the scene, and a chill went up my spine when a pair of red eyes aroused by our presence looked back at me. The serpent had a diameter of around thirty-five centimeters, and all that was wrapped around the pot. I knew when I saw it why nobody who had tried to take possession of the treasure had ever returned to their homes. This snake was a mighty specimen, and there was little doubt that it was extraordinarily strong.

The peasant didn't want to guide us down to the cave even though we'd made up our minds to do just that. I remembered that Nachita had told me that when I came face-to-face with a serpent, I couldn't show any fear and that I had to speak to it. I was willing to do that, but we couldn't get as far as that because the guide had lost his nerve. It was dangerous to head off down there without assistance; there was not only the snake to consider but the armed villagers guarding the way down.

We'd also been told that beyond our target cave, there was a buried wagon, a sort of train carriage, full of gold bars. The incredible thing was that no one had dared to take anything of value out of the wagon despite the fact that its door was at ground level. The same story applied: anyone who had tried to leave with the gold had never left the valley. The wagon could be visited but not touched. That sounded more attractive than the cave to me, but there was no convincing anyone we spoke to about helping us out. Any thought of absconding with a gold bar or two was banned by those who lived in the region.

We went from one site to another in our stay there, preferring to try to find sites that we could get to without a guide.

Hidalgo and I were driven now to an end that even we couldn't imagine. This obviously had a lot to do with not being successful after so many failed attempts. The sensation that we were getting closer all the time prevailed. We spoke about that many nights around a campfire in the forest, with nothing more than our conversation for company. But it also had a lot to do with the changes that I felt inside myself. I sensed that I had more patience and willpower than I'd ever had before, and I had a direction in my life that perhaps I had always been looking for. It was about the search for buried treasure on the one hand, but also about something much deeper as well.

We started investigating a site on a mountain where the locals said there were a lot of antique weapons and a cache of gold. It was deep in the mountain range, and getting there took its toll on my van. When we got close enough, we started climbing toward the cave but on the edge of the precipice because direct access would have been too dangerous.

The inhabitants of the closest village had told us that there wasn't enough money in the world to pay them to help us. They told us the same story that had applied to other caves that we had been to. Many went in, and few came out. They also suggested that elves were protecting the bounty and made access all but impossible. I'd never seen an elf in my life, so my curiosity was aroused by the possibility of seeing one.

We returned to Tamazunchale and went to see Don Cata. He had asked the spirit's permission to be able to travel with his diamond because on this occasion he was going to accompany us to the mountain. The diamond also had the power of enabling the viewer to see things clearly from a great distance. In the end, however, he didn't come with us but was able to pinpoint the cave's location and the presence of the bounty within. He warned us that it wouldn't be easy and gave us some money toward our expenses.

During the sinuous trek that we followed, we were sideswiped by a van coming the other way at speed. The incident happened on one of the multiple curves that we were rounding, and I was forced to swerve violently, causing the vehicle to tailspin and finish up pointing in the opposite direction. The driver of the other vehicle didn't even bother to stop and see if we were all right and drove off around the next curve. I decided to chase him; and when I caught up to him, I blew the horn madly, gesticulating for him to pull over. When he didn't do that, I accelerated around the vehicle and forced him to pull over. I obliged him to go back to his house and pay us a sum of money for the damages that the incident had caused.

This incident slowed us down considerably because we had to go first to Reynosa and then to Matamoros to get the spare parts we needed. While we were doing that, I took the opportunity to visit a local clairvoyant to tell her what we were doing and what had happened up to that moment. She advised me to keep my spirits up, but at the same time, she cast doubts on the possibility of retrieving any treasure from the site we had planned to visit and said that my future wealth would come from some other source. I wasn't too sure what she meant by that, but we bade her farewell, after which she gave us the name of another clairvoyant who she said could reveal the secret of successfully retrieving buried treasure to us. Despite the sweet promise of that, we chose to put going to the other woman on the backburner.

The jeep was going to be off the road for some time, so I bought a new car. And although it wasn't designed for rough mountain conditions, we used that from then on. Around that time, my ex-wife and my daughter returned from the United States; and I spent more time out of the house then, devoting my time to the endless search for what lay beneath the earth.

We arrived at the town and managed finally to get someone to help us. He took us to the homes of several people that knew the way to the cave, but no one was willing to guide us even with the offer of a full week's pay for only one day's work!

But we didn't let that deter us and started off on our own. The individual who had introduced us to the other locals asked us if we had good machetes, and we told him that we had those as well as a pistol if needed. I don't know what he was thinking after we told him that as we started off together.

We parked the van on a bridge over a dry riverbed and walked along a track beside the river that was splattered with large rocks and managed to reach the center of the mountain from where the climb started up to the cave. While we were walking, we heard incredibly beautiful music produced by wind instruments that seemed to come from some other forgotten time. I'd never heard anything like it before, and it seemed to be coming from the middle of the mountain.

Along the way, we saw caves inhabited by wild pigs and were careful to keep our distance because a herd of wild pigs won't hesitate to attack men regardless of how many there are. It was a dangerous trek, and we were becoming more aware of that the farther we went.

The panorama changed when we got to the slope. The track was covered by weeds and thick scrub, so we had to unsheathe the machetes and hack our way through. In this area, we were accompanied by the strange sound of what we thought must be hammers striking metal; and when we rounded a bend, we saw elves, hammers in hand, working on gold bars. They took off when they saw us and hid among the trees.

The mountain was getting dark; the clouds were low in the sky; and to our amazement, we started seeing fairies that were approximately ten to fifteen centimeters high, flying around. I thought our local helper might have left us then, but he didn't.

We continued, but strangely after we had cut our way through heavy scrub, we turned back to see that what we had hacked down had grown again! That was simply impossible.

We started cutting a new swathe through the bush, and as we did, we heard the sound of wild animals as rods of lightning started flashing through the dark sky. I sensed we were very close to what we had been looking for.

I think any other person without experience of these sorts of things would have lost their nerve then because it seemed as if we were in the middle of a horror movie full of special effects. But there was nothing fake about what was going on; it was all absolutely real!

Despite all these hardships and after finally opening the way ahead again, we got to a rocky area and felt sure that this was the point where we would find the cave that we had seen glimpses of on the way up. But to our dismay, we were wrong. I remember thinking at the time that the cave had been covered up by someone or the whole thing has been moved.

Hidalgo suggested then that if we stayed on the left side of the open area that we found ourselves in, then we might find the cave. He sensed something, that was for sure. And he was right! But when we were fifteen meters away, I realized that a slab of rock that stuck vertically out of the rock face effectively covered the entrance. That was a blow, along with the sight of fire licking its way out from within the cave. The only explanation for that that occurred to us right then was that the elves were cleaning the gold inside.

I asked the pendulum if this was our objective, and the answer was definitely yes. I asked also if we would be granted access, and the answer was a definite no! I asked the pendulum if we could eat where we were because we were starving, and it also indicated in the negative because of the surrounding danger. So we decided to start down the descent with our legs trembling from the effort and the ever-present fear of wild pigs biting into our resolve. When we got to the river, I asked the pendulum again if we could eat, and the answer was still in the negative. We had to leave immediately.

At a distance of 150 meters from the last consultation when I could see the van in the distance, we began to hear what sounded like a stampede coming our way. A quick glance over our shoulders confirmed our worst fears: a herd of wild pigs was charging toward us at incredible speed. We started sprinting for the van, but I fell over and managed to break the finger on my left hand in the fall; and then again twenty meters later, I fell again and broke another finger. I told Hidalgo that if we couldn't get to the van in time, we would have to use the machetes and the pistol.

I knew that in all probability we would be killed, but at least, we'd go down fighting.

But fortunately, we made it to the vehicle followed by the beasts that started ramming the doors after we'd jumped in. They damaged the van a bit in their wild fury, but that didn't bother me. What was more important was the fact that we'd survived. Bloodied and exhausted, we started the long drive home.

Without any doubt, that was an extraordinary experience. We heard the most beautiful music one could ever imagine hearing and saw fire coming out of a cave and then managed to just outrun a herd of wild pigs. I paid the peasant who had accompanied us well and thanked him for having helped us along the way.

On returning to Tamazunchale, we were met by Edilia, Joaquin's sister. I didn't know that she had esoteric powers; but when we met her, she said she wanted to speak with us. I told her what we'd been doing, and she wanted to know if we were going to do any more excavations. I told her that I'd had enough for the time being. But we were still going to do the odd excursion here and there, and she said she figured she could help us; so from then on, she started accompanying us into the mountains. As she was a divorced woman, the comments that flowed from our relationship were inevitable. But for me, traveling with her represented more expenses than anything else because I had to support her economically during the time she was with us. But it was good to have her there just the same. She is a woman of great courage.

Before you get to Tamazunchale, you have to pass through the town of Taman. The Cave of the American can be seen if you drive slowly along the road, but if you are driving fast, you'll miss it. When you get to the cave and take your first look at it, there appears to be a shark's jaw painted on the entrance to the cave.

The locals say that an American arrived in the region and climbed up to the cave. On entering the cave, he found a table laden with gold coins and other artifacts. No local person had entered the cave because they knew the owner of the treasure was present. The owner then appeared in front of the American and said he could take all the treasure if he gave his wife in exchange. The American agreed to that and cleaned the table of its fortune and left, never to be heard of again, and his wife died the very next day.

We were one hundred years too late when we entered that cave. Whatever had been there was long gone, and the only thing to see in its simple empty space were a few spiderwebs.

But we had other things on our mind, this time an expedition to the crags of Playa Bruja. We would need guides when we got there; but Hidalgo, Edilia, and I started off alone. We found out soon that that was a big mistake because I fell over approaching the gorge of the crags. The fall could have been fatal, but I hit the branches of a tree three hundred meters above the rocks below. Although we were carrying ropes and other equipment, we weren't tied to anything above. Either way, I was able to go back up with the help of the ropes.

After the shock of the fall, we got another surprise when we saw giant foxes beside the track to the top. I'd never seen animals like those before, and we stopped for a while to observe them. The closer we got to the cave, the more difficult the going was. Hidalgo told us that the owner of the treasure would be found in the cave, and legend had it that he lent money but wanted twice the loan paid back in gold. The borrower's family would pay with their lives if the gold wasn't handed over on time. But I wasn't interested in any of that; it was the chance of meeting El Compadre that had me really excited.

But getting into that cave was not for people who'd come unprepared. It required a descent of around two hundred meters, and our ropes only measured half of that. We tied them together and gave it a try, but there was no way we could reach the entrance. We would have to come back with special equipment or forget the idea completely.

We took photos of the cave using a zoom lens, but they were all blurred. But that was all we had for the time being and the will to try again. I had the feeling that someone was making things hard for us, almost as if we were being tested.

Sometime after that, we completed preparations for a trip to a cave in the mountains of Aman, which, according to what we'd been told, contained a large cache of treasure. Not surprisingly, we were warned about potential dangers, this time in the form of wild beasts who roamed the area around the cave. But I was prepared for any eventuality. You could say I'd become battle hardened.

We were received very strangely by the people in the small town at the foot of the mountain. They formed themselves into small groups, and as we walked past each group, they asked us what we were doing there and where we intended going. We told them straightaway what we were looking for, and one individual stepped forward and said he'd show us the way.

He took us to what amounted to more of a crack in the earth than a cave, and we were able to climb down relatively easily using our arms and legs as support. The three of us went down; but the village guide stayed where he was above because his family had arrived, and they all knew that those who went down didn't come up.

We had only been at the bottom for around twenty minutes when a landslide blocked our way back out again. Later, we were to find out that those twenty minutes inside the cave had amounted to six hours on the surface. In that time, the villagers had tried to organize a search party to come and look for us, but it consisted of people not from the village itself because none of them there were prepared to follow us down. All our time there was devoted to getting back out again, and as a result, we found nothing of any value. That's not to say that there weren't pots of gold there. Most probably, there are, but the last thing we wanted right then was to add ourselves to the list of those who had gone missing over the years. We managed to get out; and while we did that empty-handed, we learned an important lesson about the different perception of time underground.

17

The Devil's Cave

The inhabitants of this community told us about another place along the Rio Claro called the Devil's Cave. I'd tried to find the site on another occasion with Joaquin, but we'd been unsuccessful. But the villagers marked a way for us that followed a completely different route that led us directly there.

I was in a reflective mood that night before going to the cave, and while I didn't have a list of the caves and places that we had been to up to that point, it seemed a good moment to reflect on everything I'd done. The feeling of change was obvious, more than likely that was accumulative, when experience shows the way ahead or you get to a point when something tells you to give everything up. There's a big difference between being stubborn and strong-willed, and I felt right then that I had a good dose of both of those, although in which proportion, I couldn't say. And just as I was thinking that, when I went online to read something light to take my mind off other things, an e-mail from Edilia, who had stayed at home on this occasion, appeared on the screen.

She told us that she'd had a dream about finding a certain place and that we weren't able to enter it without her conducting a ritual. She detailed the ritual precisely in the body of the mail:

Look, I've bought everything that's needed for the offering, which consists of flowers, fruit, sweets, candles, incense, brandy, tequila, cigarettes, white material, gray material, red and purple ribbons, ether, mortar made of mud, water from San Ignacio de Loyola, and other waters for protection. The ritual will begin tonight, and continue for nine days and everything that is used in that time must be replaced, like the flowers, the sweets, and the incense sticks, because they are lit three times a day. The sweets are given as presents, as is the fruit, after the sessions the following day. Everything follows a plan and lasts for nine days. Some candles last days and others only hours. Everything will finish next Tuesday, and for that purpose, I need you to send me 2,000 pesos and 300 more for a black-skinned and plumed hen that I need to get on the last day. I checked the price out at a local ranch.

I also have to buy a turkey that will cost me as much as the hen; and apart from that, I have to buy pork, beef, chili, dough, butter, and salted leaves. We need all that to make a patlache or large tamal with the meat of the black hen. We'll make another smaller tamal with the feathers of the same bird and its offal. Of course, that won't be eaten; it's only buried to give thanks to the earth, which blesses us with its permission to dig. Well, that's what we're doing with the patlaches and tamales, but there's another food as well, which is sort of a red mole made from the base of seven different red chilies, and that goes with the turkey and beef and the pork. As well, I have to make boiled white rice with the stock that is made from those meats. Then I have to invite people from around the area and offer them food even though they don't know what it is. This is what the offering is all about, and as you can see, it's not that easy to put it all together. I've got to buy vases, forks, plates, serviettes, spoons. Just like I would have to if it was a great party. I'll be praying for the dead for the whole nine days. And no one will be able to help me do the cooking or light the candles during all that time. It's all very tiring, but I think it's worth it as long as everything is in place on Tuesday. If I don't do everything right, then that's another story.

Ah, I almost forgot. I've also got to buy tobacco leaves for the last day. Well, that's only part of the ritual, the part that I've just explained. The other will be what you do before entering the cave. I'll tell you all about it later, sweetheart. Everything will work out, I'm sure. I don't know if I've put everything I wanted to say in this mail. If I think of anything else, I'll send you another mail. Take care, and I hope you're pleased with everything I've just told you.

Kisses,
Edilia

It was good to know that she was devoting her time to that while we were concentrating on the physical part of overcoming the obstacles that we would confront on entering this cave. There were so many things to do; and as Edilia said in the mail, if everything isn't done just right, then the result is doomed to fail.

To enter the Devil's Cave, we had to crawl through a small opening. Inside there was a path, and from there, we had to use ropes to get down to the grotto.

At the bottom, however, we had the feeling that we were still not in the right place; and after scouting around, Hidalgo found another opening that seemed the likely way through. It was very narrow, though, and we had to spend time widening it with our tools. But in the end, common sense prevailed, and I wouldn't let Hidalgo try to crawl through because there was nothing to say that the whole thing wasn't going to collapse and leave him trapped inside.

We turned our attention to the rest of that wonderful cave. It was L shaped, and the rock walls were magnificent. Just being there produced a sensation of inner calm as if someone or something was massaging my soul.

What we were unaware of, though, was that our perception of time was vastly different to those waiting outside for us. It seemed to us that we had only been inside the cave for a half an hour or so while hours had passed outside. When we came out, they told us that they had been worried about our safety but accepted our explanation that we'd lost our sense of time in the cave.

It was another beautiful but failed expedition. But there wasn't even the slightest suggestion that we would give the whole thing away.

Before we returned home, we were told about another enchanted cave in Taman, the profile of which sounded similar to the others we'd been to: treasure and the remains of dead adventurers inside.

When we finally got home, a millionaire rancher by the name of Señor Velazquez was waiting for us. He wanted us to go to his property because, as he explained it, a rider on a great horse crossed his land every night; and Velasquez had been dreaming of late about a plot of land near some trees. We went back with him, and it didn't take me long to confirm that there was treasure buried at the site he'd been dreaming about.

I went to see Don Cata alone a few days after that. He looked in his diamond and told me immediately the value of what was buried there and its position not far from the surface. Of course, permission was required for its extraction, and something in return would have to be offered. I spoke with the rancher, and he told me he was willing to do whatever was necessary. I told him I had a few jobs that needed attending to, and after I'd done that, we would have a look at what was buried on his property. He agreed to that, and we shook hands on the deal.

That same night when I got back home, Don Torres was waiting for me. He asked me what I'd been doing because the woman from Ciudad Valles had rung him urgently to say that she'd had a vision of my death. I told him that I was spiritually dead because I had abandoned my religion but that I was physically intact as he could no doubt see and that I still had many things to do.

Torres suggested that I take special care of myself just the same and offered me his support if I needed it at any time. I told him about the places I'd been to, and he said that explained why he hadn't seen me lately in the workshop. In fact, I'd only been there on Sundays to paint and finish off work left over from the working week. I had no doubt that Torres, despite his wealth and his myriad of business activities, was curious to know what his friends were doing; and as a result of that, he worried about everyone.

I told him I was about to travel in search of the owners of certain caves in the mountains, and he confirmed that he knew the family that owned the area I'd mentioned, which made finding the property and the family a lot easier.

When I finally went there and met the owner, he told us that he would give us permission to enter the caves only on the condition that our personal safety was our responsibility. We agreed to that; and a short time later, after getting everything we needed together, one of his nephews took us to the cave entrance.

One problem we had this time around was that Hidalgo was exhausted, and everything we did seemed to take twice as long as it normally would have. Edilia was also very tired, but that wasn't my case. I felt great and ready to meet the challenge ahead. The way to the entrance surprised us because it was halfway up a slope behind some shrubs and an insignificant rock on the left-hand side.

Once we got inside the cave we found three different ways, two of which were closed; and farther down in this immense and extremely beautiful place, there was another opening.

We decided not to proceed that day because we'd been followed to the cave by a lot of people who were curious about what we were doing. We wanted to come back when things were a bit quieter than they were.

Before we left for home, we asked for and received permission to come back another day.

18

My Encounter with the Rider

T he clairvoyant in Ciudad Victoria wanted to talk with me. Don Torres informed me when he showed up at the workshop. He told me that the matter was apparently urgent, and if I didn't have anything else important to do that morning, it would be a good idea if we went there straightaway.

I rang Edilia and Hidalgo on the way to tell them that I would be away for a day or so and that they should catch up on the sleep and rest they needed after our last trek. I'm sure they appreciated that news because neither of them said they wanted to come with me to Ciudad Victoria.

The whole business of going to see the clairvoyant there at short notice seemed strange, and when she received us in her consulting room at five in the morning when we arrived, the affair became even stranger.

She seemed extraordinarily lucid for that time of the morning and explained that she had been unable to sleep because when she did finally lie down, a voice woke her up straightaway and told her that my death was imminent, although there was hope of avoiding that grim fate if I stopped what I was doing.

She asked me then what I had been doing, but I said that I would prefer her to tell me the answer to that by reading her cards. She took them out and straightaway saw a situation of conflict and war, and then she pulled the card of death out followed by triumph if my resolve stayed firm.

I asked her to read the cards again and find out if I was afraid of the supernatural, and judging by the expression on her face, the question surprised her, but she did as I asked and saw my fear in the next card but for those who were close to me.

"We're going to enter a cave that has several tunnels," I told her. "I always go in first to inspect those tunnels."

"I see war in there," she said. "Something's going to happen, and I feel that you should give the idea of going in there away."

"I'm not going to do that. I'm going right to the very end with this."

She told me then that she had done her part in telling me what she had seen; from hereon, I was on my own. She asked me to leave then, and Don Torres came in.

Torres was in there for more than an hour, and when he came out, we went to have lunch. While we were eating, he told me that the clairvoyant had spent the whole time trying to convince him to talk me out of the whole idea. She said she didn't think my heart would be able to stand the energy inside the cave.

Torres knew me well enough to know that I had no intention of doing that. Just the same, I thanked him for the concern shown, and then we drove home. He gave me money before he left to make sure I had all the right equipment for what was ahead.

Very early the next day, the architects came to my house. I was pleased to see them but surprised by their visit. Hidalgo was with them. While we were having breakfast, they told me that Nachita had sent word that we should all go and see her. She too was apparently worried for my safety.

When we went to see her, she said that a blind clairvoyant had asked to see us, and I imagined that it must have been the same one we saw when I was doing the excavation at Lupe's house.

We went to visit her, but she wasn't at home. A neighbor of the woman took us to another man, a clairvoyant, who revealed to us the latest secrets about breaking spells. I could sense this individual's power and energy. He used a glass of water and visualized things with amazing ease. He was able to tell me about my own trips and almost everything that had happened in our search for treasure. He said the first thing we had to do was follow the plan that Edilia had put forward after her dream. We needed to enact the ritual before we did anything else.

The ceremony was the same that we had done before when we entered the Devil's Cave. It would be another important expense.

We decided to pay attention to the warning about taking precautions, but he told us that although he could see that we were going to be successful, he sensed that something strange was going to happen in the cave in question.

When we arrived at the cave, a beast that seemed to be half tiger and half goat was standing at the entrance, and a giant bat was circling overhead. It walked away after a while and paid us no attention at all, so I went in but slowly, just in case the beast had had a change of mind. Inside, there was an enormous vault that led to other caverns. I sensed it was better to bring the rest of the team in so we could keep tabs on one another. I used the pendulum at all times, but it was very dark inside, and our lanterns didn't seem to be working properly. The batteries, although they were new, were nearly spent.

We started back when that happened and discovered that the way in had been sealed. We looked for another way out, and finally, Hidalgo found one. It seemed that somebody was playing games with us.

We attempted to do it again the next day, but both Edilia and Hidalgo were so exhausted that we didn't even make it to the entrance. Something strange was happening. It seemed like another visit to the clairvoyant in Valdes was in order.

That same day we left early because the drive to Valdes takes two hours. It was just as well that Torres had given me as much money as he had to cover these unforeseen events. When I got to the woman's house, she told me, "There are many spirits trying to stop you from entering the cave. But keep at it, dress in black, and make a cross of fire at the entrance and invoke these words, 'Oh, powerful Lucifer, under this cross and before you, the way of evil is closed to anything that crosses here and will never be closed again. It will remain open through the power of the four spirits of the four cardinal points that are upon the earth. So stand aside because he that is the owner of the cross has won and will do so again.'"

Just as she advised us to do, we made the cross and the oration in that cave, which measures around a meter wide and slopes down until it reaches a vault at a depth of one hundred meters and a height of fourteen meters. But at the bottom where we made the cross, there are three round cavities; and to the left of the main entrance, there is another tunnel. On this occasion, we took this left way in, which was different from our first entry. There is also a side tunnel that measures around a meter in height by a meter and a half wide. We followed it in, but there was a lot of humidity, and it was not as clear as the other sections.

We crawled military style some thirty meters with our backpacks in front of us and stayed close to the right wall so we could recognize the way back out again. We arrived in a vault, and Hidalgo cried out when we stood up, "We've done it! This is where the gold is."

Hidalgo went ahead followed by Edilia, with me bringing up the rear. There was evidence of animals having been there. The ground was marked by tracks; and there were other entrances—some small, others round—that led to other unknown vaults. Anything could happen where we were now. The bat that we had seen outside either had a brother or had followed us in. The creature had a wingspan of around two meters. I was aware of its presence, but I didn't say anything to the others because I didn't want to frighten them at that special moment because they were standing in front of the great cache of treasure that we'd been searching for all along.

We just stood there in silence, in awe of the immensity of gold before our eyes. But then, when we were so tantalizingly close to what we'd been seeking, a giant serpent, whose head was the size of my entire body, slithered out of the rear of the cave and curled itself around the treasure, and Hidalgo and Edilia froze in shock at the sight of the immense reptile.

I stepped toward the creature and said, "We don't want problems with you. We come in peace. We have brought gold coins in exchange for some of yours. So remove yourself now because we don't want to fight. Go in peace."

I stepped closer, and the serpent started to move off. (Hidalgo and Edilia didn't know that I'd brought some fake gold coins with me and that I didn't have the faintest idea what I was saying. I'd learned the art of saying nothing from Don Benito.)

We'd done it. We'd gained entry through the ritual of the cross and broken the spell, and now I'd turned the serpent away. Nevertheless, before I could put a hand on the first gold coin, a voice punctured the surrounding darkness, "How are all of you?"

We turned around to see the Rider, a tall man dressed in black. I walked some six meters toward him (the others stayed where they were, petrified out of their minds), and he extended his hand.

But I didn't follow suit. "I'm sorry but I can't shake hands. I was told not to do that."

"I can see that you haven't forgotten Don Benito's advice."

Edilia and Hidalgo were dumbfounded that I could be speaking with the Rider. It was almost as if we were speaking another language.

The Rider said, "Do you want to take some gold? You can if you want, but tell me which one of those two companions of yours you're willing to offer in return."

I told him that they weren't mine to sell. Their flesh and blood was their own, but if he allowed me to write down what we had just discussed, I would pass the page onto my friends so that any decision would then be in their hands.

He agreed to that and gave me permission to proceed.

While all this was happening, Edilia and Hidalgo stood like two statues in the background, unaware that what I had been talking about with the Rider concerned them.

I asked him then what the point was of having all the treasure stashed in this cave if it served no purpose where it was. Why keep it if he didn't need it? Why did I have to give something in return? But he simply said that everything has its price and then placed a stone with figures drawn on it in my hands. He said it recounted the story of our entire lives up to the moment we entered his cave.

He told me as well that I was the only person in the world who had got as far as this in spite of all the obstacles and tests that had been put in my way. That, he said, was perfectly natural because he was not going to permit just anyone to enter his domain. He congratulated me on my effort by saying that many others had died from the shock of seeing what I had already seen. Most of those had wanted to rob without leaving anything in exchange. He told me that one day I would have great power, that I would write this story, and that we would see each other again.

He let us go then, but it was a hasty exit because he was going to seal the site. I thanked him for allowing me to write the story, and we left in peace. As we were leaving, we turned back to see whether he was still there, but he'd vanished.

"Let's go. This is over," I said to the others as I led them away. But they said nothing as they followed me silently. I sensed that they were still in shock at what had happened.

After a while, Edilia broke her silence, "What language were you speaking to him in?"

It seemed a strange question because I had spoken in Spanish, but apparently, they had heard another language in its place.

We were moving quickly through the tunnels now as everything seemed to be coming apart. A great roar of falling rocks behind us made us sprint. We eventually got out but with great difficulty.

Once we made it outside, we were surrounded by a crowd of people. There was nothing warm about their welcome. They handcuffed us and treated us like criminals. The whole community was angry with us for having entered the mountain, and no one believed us when we said we had the permission of the owner.

We explained to them that we only had the intention of entering and looking at the gold without touching it. We had done that and left with our lives, but they insisted that they had done the same thing and lost many of their relatives. I don't know if it helped us or not, but I said that we had seen remains there that most probably belonged to their missing loved ones.

After holding us for several hours, the owner of the surrounding land arrived and told them that we had his permission to enter. They released us then, and we were allowed to leave. When we got home, I called all those who had put money into the expeditions together and told them what had happened.

They were all happy to see that I was still alive and respected the veracity of everything I told them.

Mr. Velazquez, the millionaire rancher, was very keen on unearthing the treasure on his property and was willing to do whatever was needed to that end. I told him that I would visit him later. I had no intention of doing that, but at least, it got him off my back for a while.

That same night I spoke with my staff at the workshop and told them that I was leaving and that they could have the business and the equipment, but I wanted them to relocate it somewhere else. I was going to the United States to write the story of what had happened. I didn't exactly explain that to them, but they accepted my decision without any complaint. It was a generous offer after all, and they knew it. But the events of the last few days had forced me to make this decision and shift a gear. I wasn't the same man who had opened the workshop all those years before. I felt that I had entered another stage of my life, one in which I had to obey the dictates of my instinct.

I left the town later that night, leaving everything behind. Nothing worried me now, particularly Velasquez's treasure, because I wasn't going to deliver up anyone's life for something that didn't belong to me.

As I was leaving the community, I passed a black coyote on the first curve out of town and another on the second curve and another on the third. I didn't make it as far as the fourth curve because I'd stopped the van as a sort of powerful dream invaded my mind; and a great transparent shadow entered the vehicle through the passenger door and started to twist my neck, moving it from one side to the other, causing me great pain. This shadow let me know that I had to return and gave me a final twist of my neck, which made me scream before it disappeared.

But I wasn't going to go back. I had to write the story of what had happened.

I decided to see Nachita before I left and tell her what had happened and that I was going to leave the country. She advised me to follow my feelings, that if I did that, then one day I would achieve what I wanted out of life. She also told me that after we entered the cave, several other people had done the same thing but they never saw the light of day again.

I believed that that had happened because when we were detained after leaving the cave, there had been a lot of people outside.

As can be seen after following my story as far as this, no one can enter these places without paying the consequences. There is simply too much existent energy there that is mind altering in some cases and fatal in most.

At the end of this book, you will see the stone that I was given in the cave; and you will note that in its center, there is an engraving of an angel with its wings extended. This is the main character of all the secrets of the world that I explored, the one in which I didn't belong. The photos that accompany it are the complete hierarchy of infernal spirits—Lucifer, emperor; Bezalbet, prince; and Ashtoreth, grand duke—who are the main spirits of the infernal kingdom. After them come the superior spirits who are subordinated to the former and are represented by Lucifuge, prime minister; Satanachia, grand general; Agaliareth, grand general; Fleureti, lieutenant general; Sargatanas, brigadier; and Nevirus, field marshal. These six great spirits direct their power to all other spirits.

Under their immediate orders and as special emissaries are three superior spirits—Mirion, Belial, and Anagaton—whose occupation is to transmit the orders they receive. These three have eighteen spirits subordinated to them: Bael, Agares, Marbas, Pruslas, Arimon, Barbatos, Buer, Gustatan, Botis, Batin, Pursan, Abigar, Lorai, Balefar, Foran, Aiperos, Nuberus, and Blayabolas.

The true secret of making a pact with the infernal spirits without suffering any harm is the *sanctum regnum*. The second is the *sanctum regtum*, which enables the seeker to unearth treasure without consequences.

The true sanctum regnum of the great Clavicle of Solomon is of prime importance in acquiring treasure, obtaining possession of the woman desired, discovering the most inaccessible secrets, mastering invisibility, moving to the point desired, opening all locks, and all other phenomena associated with breaking down barriers that a normal human cannot. The clavicle serves also in the forming of pacts with any of the spirits, in the manner detailed earlier in the ritual enacted at the ranch of Don Torres.

EPILOGUE

Remember on opening this book you saw a painting that symbolizes a tree in which a tiger and a child are illustrated? Well, this was painted by my ex-girlfriend in Colombia. She isn't a professional artist and paints only for pleasure, and in the time that I was with her on one of our trips together, she had a dream and related that to me when she gave me the painting.

"Do you remember that I told you what each of the figures in this painting represents?" she asked me. "Well, if you don't remember, I'll tell you again. I'll begin first with the skein of wool that is my world, still entwined but slowly unraveling as it develops. The tree has a special meaning. He who sits near a good tree is covered by good shade. There is little doubt that the tree represents something very solid in my life. It is my work or my home, or it can be both things."

She continued, "The child, my love, is you. He represents a naive person who needs to be protected and given a lot of love. And the tiger is me, a strong-spirited person, one who can protect you from everything. It is a commitment I have made because an inner voice has repeated this thought many times. The night reflects darkness and the loneliness I feel, but it also reflects the peace and tranquility that lies in my heart. I hope you'll look upon this painting with affection. It is from someone who loves you and will keep on loving you even when you are not with me."

Well, that is how she interpreted the dream that she painted; but after having read this book, you will no doubt understand my interpretation. The tree is El Compadre, and I am seated on his arm in front of the tiger, which represents the saint of death and its dangers. I am seated, although that seems strange, in the care of Lucifer because as I am the boy with his innocence exposed to the surrounding danger, I have entered a world that isn't mine: the skein (a new spiritual world), surrounded by its mysteries and dangers in which many have died.

It requires more than curiosity to walk there. Much courage and a true spiritual preparation are needed. If you do not have what is required, it would be better to not get involved in the first place because once entered, you have to be prepared to suffer the consequences.

I came back to Mexico several times in the next few years from the United States and made a few expeditions alone, without anyone knowing what I was doing. My mind was focused on finishing this book, and I didn't need anything else on my plate. I needed to talk with someone, to know why I was having so many problems finishing the work.

It was good to lose myself again on those return trips to Mexico. The jungle cleaned my mind although I didn't know that at the time. The places I went to were uninhabited, and I found my way through these remote locations by using the stars as a guide. I went to Ixtla de Santiago, Oaxaca, Puebla, and Colombia. A brief description of my trip to Oaxaca will round this story out.

FIRST TRIP TO OAXACA

I know someone in New Jersey who comes from Oaxaca, and he told me about a cave where treasure was rumored to be buried. His grandparents had stumbled upon the site when they were out hunting back in the thirties. One of the relatives of his grandparents entered that cave but didn't come out again until the following year! Everyone at the time had thought he had died inside, but he hadn't. He had simply walked out in sound physical condition. I could believe that because there is another dimension inside, and incredible energy is released by spiritual force.

And how can you prove that this is true or a lie? The answer to that is very simple. How many days did it take to create the earth? Read the Bible and find out. See how much terrestrial time equates to a single day of creation.

So I undertook the trip to Oaxaca to find this particular place. His family left me by the side of the road and told me which star to follow to find it. It wasn't easy. I spent three days walking alone; drinking nothing but water, with a few biscuits as my only source of energy; and using the pendulum to find my way.

When it looked as if I had finally arrived, at a distance some two hundred meters from the entrance, I came upon a very large tree that looked as if it had been taken from a set of a Disney film. The extraordinary thing about it was that it was completely full of white vultures, each one measuring around a meter high. They were enormous, their color made all the more striking by the fact that the tree itself was bone white. The only way to get to the cave was to pass this gloomy obstacle. The vultures were almost stationary. That's how little movement I could detect. They apparently considered me harmless. I was the one who had to worry about them.

There was no alternative but to continue. I had no machete or weapon of any kind. I felt very tired because I'd hardly slept since the trek began.

I stepped across this fearful space as the massive white birds studied me without moving their heads, watching the line of my trajectory. I managed to pass them without incident. But when I got to within ten meters of the cave, the mighty roar of a landslide inside made me stop; and straightaway, a plume of dust and stone particles shot out of the entrance. I just stood there as still as the vultures behind me, furious with the knowledge that I would never enter that cave.

I stayed there wandering around, looking at the hillside and the mountains above. It was midday. I could perceive a sense of fear in me because I didn't know how to return. I was totally lost. After a while, however, I got control of myself and pulled the pendulum out, put it to work, and regained my sense of direction and returned via another route.

I arrived at the edge of the road a day later; and behind me, in an area devoid of people, I was followed by a white wolf. He had been there all the way, and he looked very tired. Twenty meters from the road, there was a small altar that had been put there to honor the memory of some people who'd died in an accident. The little chapel threw out a large shadow thanks to its slate roof.

The wolf lay down right there, and I decided to sit down too. But when I went to take off my backpack and turned around again, the animal was gone. He simply disappeared. At that point, I could see for a half a mile in every direction. But it didn't matter which way I looked—there was no sight of him. There was nothing there at all. After twenty minutes of sitting there confused but resting as much as I could, I saw a car drive up with none other than my friend's father sitting behind the steering wheel. He told me later that they all felt guilty for having let me go off hiking on my own in the mountains. He also told me that when I had begun the trek, they had seen a very tall man wearing a black hat and clothes walking beside me. I hadn't seen anyone, of course. But they had. It seems that I hadn't been alone at all on that strange walk through the mountains.

On my return to the United States, I spoke with a friend of mine who has the gift of being able to speak face-to-face with El Compadre every Tuesday and Thursday, and I asked him to ask Lucifer why I hadn't been allowed to enter that cave. The simple answer was that I was being put through another test.

The following year I was told about another large grotto that was two hours of dirt track driving past Putla de Oaxaca. I went there following the information that a friend had given me. One curious requirement for entering this cave was the fact that I needed to fast for three days, which was something I had started two days before my arrival.

The owner of the property on which the cave was located told me that if anyone asked me who I was and what I was doing there, I should tell them that I was his nephew. He was concerned that the local people might resent my presence to such an extent that they might attack me. It was a very primitive, lawless area, and it was better to have your story right before you got there.

The following photo is of a relative of the owner of the property who guided me to the cave. In the photo, he appears to be around sixty years old; but in fact, he is eighty. This man was incredibly strong, and his ability with a machete was astonishing. I would never have got there without him, mainly because the area was infested with snakes. I've never seen anyone kill reptiles like this man did. His hearing was that acute that he could hear the faintest slither in the undergrowth.

Another image of the area.

The eighty-year-old left me there at midnight because that was the time designated for entry. Before he left, he asked me if I was sure that I wanted to go in because he knew that the owner of all treasure was inside and that I could easily die from shock within those walls. I told him not to worry because I knew what I was doing.

He chuckled at my comment because he couldn't believe that someone from the capital like me could be entering a place of such force and energy like the one I was about to go into. Nobody from the region would do what I was doing.

He left me then, and I felt emptiness invade me. He was a strong man with a lot of experience. Crossing that dangerous land that had led me to the cave had been very hard indeed. And I had felt protected with him being at my side. But now I was alone. I watched him disappear around a corner of the forest track and felt a chill enter the pit of my stomach. But I snapped out of that mood straightaway and concentrated on the job in hand.

I had to cut a hole in the barricade that the locals had used to block the entrance. It was a pity that they'd done that because it was a wonder of nature inside that cave. There was a lake and antique carriages and a host of bewitched animals (horses, sheep, etc.); and even more impressive than that was the castle inside the cave with relics from the time of the Aztecs and weaponry from the era of the Mexican Revolution.

There was also a large round stone, no doubt a sacrificial altar, some ten meters in diameter.

At the entrance to the castle, in a small anteroom, there was an abundance of gold and jewels that had been curiously kept clean. There wasn't a speck of dust on the gold bars and gems. All that was already strange enough before I heard a hollow voice behind me.

I was so absorbed in everything that I was looking at that I had forgotten that a king lives in a castle or, as legend states, a Minotaur in a labyrinth. I came back to reality with a thud and span around on my heels. Introductions weren't necessary. I got straight to the point and asked him why I hadn't been able to publish my book yet, and he answered that I needed to be patient. I asked him permission then to take photos, and as there was no reply to the question, I started taking them. But to my later surprise, none of the photos taken in the cave came out. All I had were the photos of my approach to and my leaving of the cave.

El Compadre said nothing more other than "Go home. Now we have seen each other."

And with that, everything finished.

At the beginning of my adventures, I had an accident and broke some ribs, and they set a millimeter or so out of place. I remember that I was sleeping in my bed around midnight one night when suddenly I heard someone kicking the door. The noise was that loud that I woke up and stared at the door in silence. I sensed that someone had entered the room, and I was waiting until whoever it was got closer before I did anything. But then, I felt his energy. I knew that it was him, and in the moonlight reflected on the wall, I saw another light and an angel. I was lying on my side, and a lilting female voice said, "Don't move, or I'll bite you hard."

But what was bitten was the pillow. I bit it as she began to strike me repeatedly on the ribs, putting them back in place.

The pain was that intense that I couldn't help but scream and wail, and when it was over, all I heard was a final word of advice: "Don't work for a week." And then she was gone.

I asked some clairvoyant friends of mine what the reason could be for having had my ribs fixed without me having asked or prayed for any assistance. The answers were more or less the same: I had to be in good condition for my future journeys.

The second meeting was when I was suffering from kidney problems and was urinating blood. I knew that if I went to a hospital in the United States, the attention would cost me a lot, so I decided to return to Mexico. And at midnight the first night back, he presented himself but in the same form as the previous occasion.

The angel told me, "Turn over." And I started to see waves of energy reflected on the wall again as I was struck in the lower back, and a while later, I heard, "Finished—kidney, pancreas, and liver repaired."

My friends told me the same thing as before. I was being kept in optimum condition for future trips.

So with these few examples of what have taken place in my life after I left Mexico, I will finish this story up to the present. I would like once more to thank everyone who has made the publication of this book possible. Only one of those mentioned in these pages has passed away. The rest are still alive.

All inquiries should be directed to the following e-mail address:

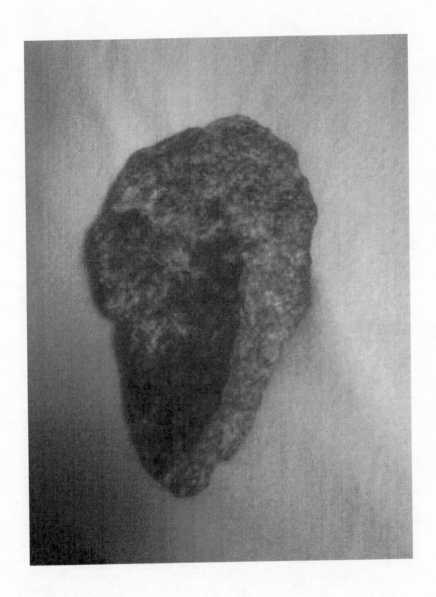

INDEX

Z

Printed in the United States
By Bookmasters